Paddy O'Brien was born in Gateshead in 1953. She runs a personnel training consultancy specialising in women's development work and stress management. Trained in Tae Kwon Do with Meng Ken Too (Korean 5th Dan) and Mark Biddlecombe (UK 2nd Dan). She has recently begun to train with Master Han (Korean 6th Dan) of Hwarang Do, Slough. Paddy runs self-defence classes for women's and mixed groups of professionals in hazardous work. She is Personal Safety Consultant for the Pepperell Unit of the Industrial Society, and has also practised and taught yoga for many years. She lives near Windsor with her partner and children.

OPTIMA

AN INTRODUCTION TO TAE KWON DO

PADDY O'BRIEN

ILLUSTRATED BY SU EATON

An Optima book

First published in 1991 by
Macdonald Optima, a division of
Macdonald & Co. (Publishers) Ltd

A member of Maxwell Macmillan Publishing Corporation

British Library Cataloguing in Publication Data

Macdonald & Co (Publishers) Ltd
165 Great Dover St
London
SE1 4YA

Typeset by Leaper & Gard Limited, Bristol
Printed and bound in Great Britain by
The Guernsey Press Co. Ltd, Guernsey, Channel Islands.

DEDICATION

This book is dedicated to D.P. O'Brien and his fighting spirit.

CONTENTS

PREFACE

This book is an introduction to, and a reflection on, tae kwon do. I hope it will be both a good source book of basic information and a catalyst for new insights for students involved in this particular Way.

The book contains suggestions for body conditioning and mental and spiritual preparation, as well as information about basic technique, patterns and sparring. There is discussion of the modern meaning of *budo*, the Way of the warrior, as it is expressed in tae kwon do, as well as description of the historical background to the art.

ACKNOWLEDGMENTS

I must thank Robbie Lazan of Hwarang Do in Slough for his assistance with the chapter on the roots of tae kwon do.

My teachers have been Meng Ken Too of Chung Do Kwan, Korea and Southampton, and Mark Biddlecombe of Southampton City Tae Kwon Do Chung Do Kwan. Very recently I have joined the class of Master Han of Hwarang Tae Kwon Do in Slough. To their inspiring teaching I owe any skill and perception you find in this book.

Any shortcomings are of course entirely my own.

1
INTRODUCTION

In Buddhism there are three kinds of giving: giving materials, giving teachings (Dharma), and giving fearlessness. (*Returning to Silence*, Dainin Katagiri)

WHAT IS TAE KWON DO?

Tae kwon do means the art of kicking and punching. It is a Korean martial art whose origins stretch back 2,000 years, and is now practised by over 18 million people in 80 countries across the world. This is an art of great range and contrasts: there are the spectacular and beautiful techniques, including the breathtaking leaping and flying kicks, originally evolved to enable a fighter on foot to unseat a warrior on horseback; and astonishing breaking techniques, in which soft human hands and feet pass unscathed through seemingly unyielding bricks, roof tiles and blocks of wood. These dramatic exercises are perhaps the most visible and memorable aspects of the art to people who are not actually involved in studying it; and are of course important and enjoyable. They are, however, only a part of the study of tae kwon do. The work also includes long and patient practice of basic technique – ordinary kicks, strikes and punches, repeated over and over again, week in, week out, class in and class out, looking for the equilibrium, the shape, the power and the precision to which every student eventually aspires.

Revisiting the shape and form of the front kick, side kick, knife-hand strike, hammer fist and all the other basic techniques forces you, time after time, to face yourself at that particular moment on that particular day. How is your mood, your integration, your circulation, your digestion, your weight, your power, your spirit? The

Deemyun yop-cha jireugi, flying side kick.

answers to these questions are soon revealed when you get on to the floor of the *dojang* and begin to inhabit the familiar moves. You cannot lie to yourself; you know how you are. Time after time you face the choice; either you have to re-integrate your energies and move into growth and change, or you stay as you are and don't take up the challenge to grow and move on.

Similar choices face the student practising forms. Forms are beautiful to watch, as aesthetically pleasing as any contemporary dance. Performing forms is a process of fighting a battle with imaginary enemies who attack from every side. To move through the form convincingly, one visualizes the opposing warriors moving in with attacks, which one blocks, and then counter-attacks. The space around, although empty, is full of the projected energies of an attacking force. The practitioner is in his own world. The attacking force may have many meanings for him. It might represent literal physical attackers, or what Sun Tzu's translator R.L. Wing calls 'environmental' enemies (i.e. the organization you work for, the partnership you inhabit, the political regime you live in), or the attackers within that all of us must at times contend with – self-destruction, self-doubt, self-hatred or inertia. In the form, the student studies ways of defeating an enemy of whatever kind.

The beauty of tae kwon do forms: *Taeguek* four, *sah jang*, position 5.

The same 'enemy' appears in prearranged sparring and free sparring. Nobody consciously projects the identity of a hated person or institution, or a hated aspect of themselves, on to their sparring partner, but one may notice in retrospect that some sort of process of 'fighting out' internal conflicts has indeed been happening. In prearranged sparring, sequences of attack and defence are repeated until they flow like a smooth reflex reaction, the students in pairs taking turns to play the attacking and defending role. At the white-belt beginning level the sequences are simple, although still very powerful. Moving up through the grades, students learn increasingly elaborate sequences, incorporating increasingly demanding techniques, although still accomplished within two or three steps. Body and mind are educated into responding swiftly and without stress in a wide variety of ways to attack.

In free sparring, students fight in pairs without prearranged moves. Rounds last between two and three minutes, and are extremely demanding, both mentally and physically. Stamina is essential in order to enable you to keep moving quickly and lightly, to continue to unleash techniques, including head-high kicks. But strategy is equally important, allowing you to respond to the strengths and weaknesses of an opponent, and to pace your energy and rhythm. In training sessions, students fight with no contact or light contact, putting full commitment into every technique, but pulling the technique at the last possible moment. Free sparring thus confronts the student with his or her own fear, and puts them in touch with their own fierceness and determination.

So tae kwon do embodies aesthetic and spectacular work, as well as a solid foundation of basic technique. It includes form and symmetry in patterns, and ferocity and unpredictability in sparring. These are, in turn, balanced by the peace and steadiness of the meditation that is also part of the discipline; students learn to empty the mind and reflect on the spirit in stillness and quiet.

The paradoxical nature of these qualities show how the yin and the yang, the opposites of 'feminine' and 'masculine' energy, are represented in the art. The yin/yang sign

The Korean flag.

is at the centre of the Korean flag, which is always pinned up in the tae kwon do *dojang.* It shows how opposing energies must exist in fluid balance with one another, and how each quality contains within itself the seed (represented by the small dot) of the opposite energy. Tae kwon do (the Way of the foot and the fist), as with so many other disciplines – judo (the gentle way), aikido (the Way of spirit harmony), karate-do (the Way of the empty hand), kyudo (the Way of the bow), chado (the Way of tea), shado (the Way of calligraphy), kado (the Way of flowers) – is a Way or Way of life (Korean *do,* Japanese *do* and Chinese *tao* all mean Way) that attempts to integrate the yin and the yang. This explains why the more knowledge and understanding that students gain, the less aggression and ego they will have. Anyone arriving at class in an aggressive and violent frame of mind will either leave fairly quickly, realizing their violence cannot be indulged in this context, or, if they stay, will actually become gentle and compassionate in direct ratio to the skills that they attain. Unless it is very unscrupulously taught, there is no question of tae kwon do technique feeding into and increasing anybody's violence. Because of the yin/yang paradox, the person becomes less angry, less arrogant and less violent.

However, tae kwon do also has an everyday face – the repetitive practice of basic kicks, basic punches, basic strikes; the feeling of getting nowhere; the feeling of comradeship with other class members. One does not consciously struggle for enlightenment: one struggles to get a kick or a punch correctly performed. These cumulative efforts may or may not lead to enlightenment, but most of the time it is the daily effort, the daily frustration, the occasional exhilaration, which the student is most conscious of. Getting fitter, becoming more flexible, overcoming technical difficulty with movements, and enjoying the effort (and suffering) shared with other students, is the basic experience of attending class.

WHO CAN TAKE PART?

Almost anyone can take part in tae kwon do, because a good teacher will be aiming to help each student improve in his or her own way and achieve their own full potential at their own appropriate pace. While there should be a spirit of commitment and endeavour in the training session, there should not be a spirit of competitiveness since this can only artificially inflate the egos of some participants, while artificially disempowering others.

Children under the age of eight or so may find it difficult to concentrate through a one-and-a-half-hour training session, and it may be more appropriate for youngsters under the age of 12 or 14 to train in a separate junior class, where a different approach and pace of instruction can be used. However, some instructors find benefits in a class that has a mixture of children and adults because it brings out patience and consideration in the adults, makes the children more inclined to take responsibility for themselves, and develops tolerance all round. And in a small club it may be impossible to run separate classes for different age groups, in which case the instructor will have little alternative but to integrate them. Children should not be allowed to attempt breaking techniques, though, because of the potential damage to still-developing bones and joints.

At the other end of the age range, both men and women in late middle or old age should be aware that their bones become increasingly brittle, and for this reason they may not feel that it is appropriate to take part in full contact combat of any kind. Nevertheless, so long as fitness and flexibility are built up slowly and progressively (particularly if the student was not fit before becoming involved in tae kwon do), there is no reason why an older person should not gain a great deal from, and contribute a great deal to, tae kwon do. In fact, the practice of this or any other physical discipline or sport helps to maintain bone and muscle mass, and so is positively beneficial to anyone of middle age or over, who will begin to lose this bone and muscle mass unless they lead a physically vigorous life.

Women students of tae kwon do may feel particularly challenged during their periods, and wonder what they should do about training during pregnancy. In both these cases the choice must be up to the individual. Some women find it useful to take supplements such as vitamin B6, vitamin C or brewer's yeast, around the time of their period, in order to counteract the cyclical fluctuations in energy and mood. If you feel you might want a vitamin or iron or other nutritional supplement, discuss it with your GP, describing training and your difficulties with energy levels, rather than buying supplements at random yourself. Alternatively, it may be possible to adjust your diet rather than take supplements.

The other way of looking at the variation of energy is to see it as a part of a rhythm, and a positive opportunity to practise flowing with something, rather than resisting it by tensing up. Unless your cycle is very disruptive and makes you feel positively weak and ill, it seems more coherent with the philosophy of martial arts to learn to be sensitive and responsive to the cycle itself, knowing it is an example of the yin and yang variable balances within you as the weeks pass.

Current medical research suggests that a healthy pregnancy will be unharmed in the first trimester, even by rigorous training. So if you become pregnant, and have not suffered miscarriage or other complications of pregnancy before, it is all right to continue training for the first 12 weeks of the pregnancy, although you should not do any prearranged or free sparring as you must avoid any risk of a direct blow to the abdomen. However, if you have had problems with fertility, or have experienced previous miscarriages, you may prefer to stop training, on the commonsense basis that taking life easy must be protective to the pregnancy. And if you feel low abdominal cramp while training in early pregnancy, this also is a signal from your body that it is time for you to take life more slowly, and that it would be better to stop full training.

After the 12th week of pregnancy the uterus begins to

rise up out of the pelvis, and is therefore more vulnerable; most women feel that this is the time to move into a more moderate physical programme. For example, hatha yoga can be practised throughout pregnancy (see *Birth and Our Bodies* – details under Further Reading at back of book), and is an ideal way to maintain flexibility and a certain level of strength until you are able to train in tae kwon do again. The philosophical basis of yoga is the same as that of tae kwon do, and so is a good sister discipline to the martial arts. Once you have begun yoga you will probably want to continue with it anyway.

The length of time it takes to recover fitness after you have had a baby depends on how fit you were before you became pregnant, how the birth itself went and how much time you are able to find to exercise afterwards. The main thing is not to panic if, a couple of days after the birth, you feel you will never again manage a jumping reverse crescent kick: it is a very reasonable thought to have at this stage; and you will manage it again. The key is to rebuild your strength and fitness gradually. Start with a progressive programme (such as *Post Natal Exercises*), keep your yoga going, and gradually rebuild aerobic and muscular fitness with an aerobic tape or class, or low repetitions of the usual tae kwon do warm-up exercises. When you feel ready, start to walk through the *taeguek* forms, and then to practise them with increased power. Once you can manage a standard aerobic class, and comfortably practise forms, you are ready to return to class. Do not worry if it takes three or four months to arrive at this stage; it is better to rebuild your strength slowly and steadily than to rush it and risk injury and the accompanying disappointment and setback. Have faith in your body's ability to become strong at its own pace.

The courage and strength needed in childbirth – and in looking after a baby – will give a new toughness to your practice and attitude. The real depth of female power is described by Lao Tsu in *Tao Te Ching* (The Way of Power):

The valley spirit never dies;
It is the woman, primal mother.
Her gateway is the root of heaven and earth.
It is like a veil barely seen.
Use it; it will never fail.

Medical conditions and tae kwon do

If you are asthmatic, practising tae kwon do will be of positive benefit to you because it will increase your lung capacity. If you use an inhaler, use the correct dose before the class begins, so that you do not get out of breath.

If you are diabetic you need to assess how much energy you will expend at class and adjust your insulin/sugar levels, and take a supply of sugar with you to the *dojang* in case you need any extra.

Tae kwon do training may be beneficial to a person with minor heart problems, but it must be practised in moderation, with due attention to any discomfort in the chest or breathlessness, and with medication always brought to the session and kept to hand. Anyone who has a cardiac condition or any worries about their heart should have a medical, and discuss their proposed training with their GP before starting to attend class.

People with haemophilia are part of the small minority who really should never train in tae kwon do. Because of the lack of the clotting factor in their blood, the smallest injury can start a serious bleed, and even vigorous warm-up and basic technique practice can cause small internal muscular tears which may bleed.

WHAT ARE THE BENEFITS?

The demanding training of the tae kwon do session benefits all the physical systems of the body. Cardiovascular and lung functions are enhanced by the stamina-building aspects of the training, both the anaerobic elements (short sprints, working muscle groups to exhaustion, and fast and furious free sparring) and the aerobic work (when muscles are worked repeatedly but not to their limit of endurance, so that breathing and pulse rate are raised, but not to extreme levels). Muscles increase in strength, and muscles and joints develop a greater range of movement and flexibility, both because of the stretching exercises performed during the warm-up and because of the scope of movement involved in the techniques themselves.

The energetic exercise and extensive stretching improve lymphatic drainage, which is essential to the functioning of the immune system, and therefore boost the body's general health. The focused and committed physical effort expended at training at least twice a week will help dispel insomnia, and this effort will also use up the excesses of adrenalin that our stressful but non-physical lifestyle tends to accumulate in our systems. Furthermore, the production of endorphins – body chemicals that raise the pain threshold and give a feeling of well-being – is also encouraged.

The student who practises tae kwon do will experience an overall growth in confidence and courage, even though there may be plenty of occasions when one feels scared, inadequate, or uncertain as to how to progress. Insight into the self and others deepens, and with it an ability to defend and maintain oneself emotionally. Clearly the ability to defend yourself physically in a last resort against violent attack is a valuable skill, but the true lesson of tae kwon do, as of all the other martial arts, is wherever possible the complete avoidance of violence.

So, to return to the beginning of the chapter, the three types of giving in tae kwon do are: the techniques themselves, which are the materials; the teachings, which are the insights and philosophy; and, finally, operating at many levels, the gift of fearlessness.

2 PREPARING THE BODY

> Poise your body like a hawk ... walk like a cat. (Wang Chung Yueh)

Preparing the body for tae kwon do involves developing flexibility, increasing stamina and increasing strength. Although each of these elements could constitute a discipline and a goal in itself, tae kwon do demands an awareness and sensitivity such that you balance your training in order to get your body into its best possible condition for this particular art.

You can overdo any of the three. For example, although it is probably impossible to become too supple, two cautions must apply to stretching. One is an obvious commonsense point, which is to avoid an excess of zeal that might lead you to over-stretch to the point of injury. The other is a more subtle point, and one that I have sometimes been guilty of myself; the deep stillness arrived at in the body by stretching in the yoga manner, while excellent for meditation and for developing an extensive flexibility, can tip over into a kind of inertia or trance-like state from which one has to shake oneself free in order to get the right sort of energy into techniques.

Some resistance training is useful, as it increases localized muscle power; but most people find that when muscles start to bulk up more than moderately, some flexibility is lost. Again it is a question of balance, for a certain amount of such training will increase the power and definition of techniques, and discourage the sorts of faults that arise when stronger muscle groups are 'carrying' or compensating for weaker parts of the body, making for an imbalanced overall execution of the technique.

Stamina training is essential, both to build up the reserves of energy needed for sparring and to raise your general level of physical endurance. But if you do work hard on stamina, be aware that running beyond a certain limit may place too much wear and tear on hip, knee and foot joints, and may also result in more than an ideal weight loss.

These cautions and reservations should therefore show you that it is important to orchestrate the different kinds of preparatory training so that you arrive at that balance in your own body in which you can best practise tae kwon do.

There follow some suggestions for basic preparatory exercises.

STRETCHING

Always respect your own limits when stretching – becoming impatient or angry and over-stretching will merely lead to injuries that can be tediously slow to clear up. Learn to recognize the physical sensations that indicate when you are working hard enough to encourage the muscles to stretch, and be aware of the moment when they change and warn you of the risk of strain. Move slowly and smoothly into the stretches, and equally smoothly and slowly out of them – it is just as easy to injure yourself coming out of a movement awkwardly as it is going into one awkwardly, a point that is sometimes forgotten.

Ideally, you should do some stretching every day. If you feel under too much pressure to find time for this, choose one stretch for each direction (forward bend, back bend, side bend, leg stretch and twist), and make these stretches slowly and attentively. It will only take five or ten minutes, but will make a surprising amount more space in your body.

Head, neck and shoulders

Many of us collect a great deal of tension in the head, neck and shoulders. Sedentary work – sitting over a desk or a computer terminal – predisposes us to this, as well as to many other postural tensions and misalignments. Pressure of work and emotional stress also create tension in the neck and shoulder muscles.

While executing tae kwon do technique the head should be poised and not shaken around. The back of the neck should be long – a lifting extension of a supple spine; you should avoid contracting the neck and jutting the chin out, while the shoulders should be relaxed and poised. To achieve this balanced state of relaxed readiness, the neck and shoulders must be regularly stretched and opened, and always warmed up before any technique is practised. To establish the habit of a good head position while training, simply remind yourself to keep the back of your neck long.

Stand with the spine lifting, abdomen lifting, and your shoulders relaxed back and down. Inhale, then, as you exhale, slowly drop your head forwards, so your chin is on your chest. Link your hands and rest them on the back of your head; let the forearms come down, elbows pointing to the floor, so that the weight of your arms helps your neck stretch. Keep a steady rhythm of breathing, your spine lifting, your body upright. After a few seconds inhale, release your hands and let your head float back to the centre. Then, as you exhale, let your head fall back; think of stretching your throat and making long rather than snapping your neck back. Breathe steadily, then after a few seconds inhale and float your head back up to the centre.

Check your stance is still upright, relaxed but alert. Put your hands in *choonbi* position. On an exhalation, drop your right ear down towards your right shoulder, lengthening the left side of your neck. Breathe steadily. After a few seconds inhale and raise your head to the centre, then exhale and drop it to the other side, elongating the right side of your neck, and breathing steadily. After a few

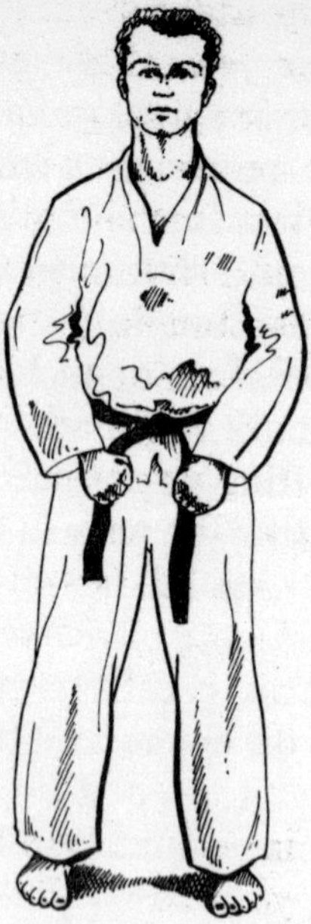

Choonbi stance.

seconds, on a breath in, float your head back up to the centre.

Now, exhaling, drop your chin on to your chest and, breathing steadily, circle your head slowly twice in one direction, then twice in the other direction. Keep your spine lifting, your abdomen lifting, your shoulders relaxed and poised. Raise your head back to the centre when you finish.

Open your shoulders, step your feet twice your hip-distance apart and link your hands behind your back. Inhaling, stand tall, then on the exhalation stretch forwards as far as you can, hinging the body at the top of the thighs, then stretch down, letting your arms stretch out above your back. Breathe steadily. Experience the stretch up the backs of your legs, and feel your chest, shoulders and upper arms stretching. Do not bounce. Let your head be heavy, your neck long, and think of making your spine as long as you can. After a few seconds, inhale and lift your head up, and carefully rest your arms on your back again; then, as you exhale, press your abdomen up and back towards your spine, press your feet into the floor and come back into an upright position.

Warm the shoulders further by standing tall, your feet hip-distance apart, and sliding your left hand up between your shoulder blades. Inhaling, stretch your right arm up into the air, and, exhaling, bend it at the elbow and reach down to catch your left fingertips; at first it may be difficult even to touch fingertips, but eventually you will be able to hold on to opposite wrists. Hold for a few seconds, breathing steadily, then inhale and stretch the right arm up; exhaling, rest it down and slide the left arm down again too. Repeat this stretch to the other side; you may be surprised at the difference in ease or difficulty between the two sides.

Be aware of an important point about symmetry. You will tend to make your best effort on the side you start with; many of us therefore become very right-sided, since this is the side which we begin with conventionally. So remember to compensate for this either by sometimes electing to practise on the left side first, or by sometimes deliberately spending more time and concentration on work on the left side. Alternatively, always try to focus equally on each side and thus avoid developing an imbalance or exaggerating an imbalance that is already there.

The shoulders can be further loosened and warmed by swinging the arms forwards loosely in circles, backwards in circles, and by rolling the shoulders forwards and then backwards in a relaxed circular motion. Keep the spine poised and upright and the abdomen lifting all the time, and equal weight on each foot. Shoulders and chest can be loosened and opened by crossing the arms across the chest and then flinging them loosely back. This simple exercise is good for opening up the spirit too. Tension and stress cause us to tense up and close the chest as well as the back of the neck; movements that enhance free and open flow across the front of the chest cause you literally and metaphorically to 'open your heart'.

Waist and abdomen

Stretching and extending in the waist and abdomen involves twisting, side-stretching and back-bending stretches. It is important to keep the waist and abdomen supple, as well as strengthening the muscles with power exercises (see page 25), as free and fluent movement in the mid-section of the body is vital to bringing life and power into tae kwon do techniques.

To perform a side stretch, stand with your feet parallel one-and-a-half hip-distances apart; tuck the tailbone under, lift the abdomen, lengthen the neck and stand tall. Exhaling, and keeping the body all in one plane, slide your right hand down your right leg as far as possible, chest and hips facing the front. Hold with steady breathing for a few seconds, then breathe in and come up. Make the same stretch on the left side, with equal concentration, for an equal length of time, then inhale and come up. Increase this stretch by repeating it a few more times each side with the upper arm stretched over your head, elbow bent, hand in a loose fist.

Side stretch.

Side stretch with a partner.

Side-stretching can be performed with a partner. Stand with your feet wide apart, facing in the opposite directions, and line up the outside edges of your inside feet. Join your inside hands at waist level, outside hands up and over your head, then, on an exhalation, bend the outer knees. Bounce gently to increase the stretch. Breathing in, come up, then change sides and work with equal concentration on the other side.

Mid-section flexibility

The waist and hips can be loosened and warmed further by circling the hips in large slow circles, feet hip-width apart and hands on hips. Then step the feet wide apart and, flopping forwards from the waist, circle the whole body round a few times in each direction.

A back-bending sequence lengthens and opens the front of the body while also increasing flexibility in the spine. Begin by lying on your stomach on the floor, palms down and fingers pointing forwards on the floor at shoulder level. Turn your face to the floor and inhale, then, as you breathe out, lift the upper body up off the floor like a snake, keeping your pubic bone in contact with the floor. If you come up far enough, drop your head back and open your chest further, but do not let your shoulders push up into your ears. Hold for a few seconds, breathing steadily, then, exhale and uncoil yourself down on to the floor. Rest your face on one side for a few seconds.

Now, move your hands down to chest level, still with the palms facing down and the fingers pointing forwards. Turn your face to the floor once more and inhale. As you exhale, lift your upper body up off the floor again, keeping your pubic bone on the floor. If you come up far enough, drop your head back and open your chest further, again without pushing your shoulders up towards your ears. Hold for a few seconds, breathing steadily, then, exhaling slowly lower down on to the floor.

Repeat one last time, this time with hands at belt level. After this push up on to your hands and knees, and then sit back on your heels, elongating your spine and with your hands and arms stretched forward. This relieves any feeling of compression in your lower back.

A more intense back bend can be experienced by forming a bridge, or what children call a crab. Lie on your back, knees bent, feet flat on the floor near your hips. Bend your arms back so that you can rest your palms on the floor, with your fingers pointing down towards your heels. On an exhalation push up into an arch, taking your weight on your feet and your hands. Hold for a few seconds, breathing steadily. When you come down, exhale and lower your body slowly and with control, then hug your knees on to your chest to eliminate any feeling of constriction. Repeat the stretch again, moving into it and out of it smoothly and carefully. You can feel that it opens and stretches the front of the body while giving the spine an invigorating back bend, and strengthening your wrists and forearms.

When you become very strong and confident in this stretch, try bringing one leg, knee bent, up on to your chest, then extending the leg straight into the air. Hold for a few seconds, breathing steadily, then bring the leg down and do the same on the other side. A further variation, once your confidence has increased, is to walk your hands backwards down a wall until you arrive in the back arch position, and you may eventually be able to drop straight backwards into the back arch. But do not attempt either of these variations until you feel ready, and always have a friend ready to catch you the first few times you try.

Twisting stretches can be incorporated into many of the sitting stretches intended primarily to work on the legs and spine (e.g. pages 21 and 22), simply by crossing an arm across the front and turning to twist in the direction of its leverage. Always visualize a twisting spiral movement originating in the base of the spine and moving up through it; by doing this you will execute a more profound twist, and also avoid the type of injury that can be caused by violent localized twisting around the waist. Twist on an exhalation, and be aware of keeping your spine and abdomen lifted and lengthened as you make the twisting movement. Hold each stretch for a few seconds, breathing steadily, and come out of the stretches slowly and carefully.

Spine, legs and hips

Many stretches facilitate extension in, and promote flexibility of, the spine, legs and hips. But in all forward bending and stretching exercises remember two points: keep the front and back surfaces of the body as open and as free as possible (i.e. avoid hunching the back or crumpling up the abdomen); and visualize the hinge where you bend being at the top of the thighs, not at the back of the waist.

From a standing position, with your feet twice shoulder-width apart, on an exhalation stretch your face down towards your right knee. Hold it there, breathing steadily, experiencing the stretch in the back, hip and the back of your right leg. Inhale and lift your head; exhale and come up. Repeat to the other side, this time feeling a stretch in the left leg as well as the back and hip. Come up methodically on this side too.

Stretching the thighs and hamstrings.

With your feet still twice shoulder-width apart, drop the upper body forward and down to the centre, hold on to the opposite elbows and think, eventually, of bringing your elbows to the floor (this may seem a long way away when you first begin stretching, but it will eventually happen). Hold the stretch for a few seconds, breathing steadily. To come up, inhale and lift your head, then exhale and press the abdomen up and back towards the spine to lift your body up.

The next stretch begins to work on the abduction of the thighs as well as stretching the hamstrings. With your left leg extended to the side, toes pointing upwards, squat down with the right leg bent, right hand on the floor in front, left hand on the floor behind, for balance. Look towards your left toes and hold the stretch, breathing steadily.

Now change sides, pushing into your feet to stand up and coming down on the other side, this time stretching the right leg out straight. Use the elbow of the front arm to open the knee more. Hold for an equal length of time on this side.

Move back to the first side again, with the left leg out straight. Making fists with the hands, arms extended in front of the body for balance, change from side to side fairly quickly a few times. This builds up strength in the thighs and calves as you push your weight up and over to each side.

Working towards box splits, stand with your feet as far apart as feels safe (there is no point in forcing this, as injury in the groin or inner thigh is inhibiting to training and slow to heal). Rest your hands on your hips or upper things, then, as the muscles warm up, allow your feet to spread further apart. Stretch forwards and take your weight on your hands, pressing your hips down towards the ground, then perform a few rolling press-ups, rolling the hips forwards, then taking the weight on to your hands and forearms and pushing up. You will feel the stretch in your hips and legs gradually increasing.

Now place one hand on the floor in front of your hips, and the other on the floor behind. Make small rocking movements with your hips to increase your stretch still more, then sit down (with control, don't collapse), and lift up from the base of your spine to the crown of your head. Make loose fists and massage the inner thigh muscles by striking them, then massage the knees with circular stroking movements with the palms of the hands – a few times in each direction.

Turn to look along your right leg. Inhale and stretch your spine upwards, then exhale and stretch out along the top of your leg. Think of getting your chest towards your knee rather than your forehead on to your knee. Hold for a few seconds, breathing steadily, then inhale, lift your head, and, exhaling, sit up straight. After checking that your spine and abdomen are lifting, turn to face along the other leg and repeat the forward stretch on the other side, with equal concentration.

Return to the centre. Inhaling, lift and stretch the body, then stretch forwards and down, again thinking of getting your chest rather than your forehead on to the floor. For most people it takes many months of stretching before it is possible to reach the full extent of this stretch. After holding for a few seconds with steady breathing, inhale and come up.

A different part of the inner thigh is loosened by

bringing the soles of the feet together and allowing the bent knees to fall out to the sides. Clasp your hands around your feet and stretch your spine upwards in order to get the maximum benefit from the stretch. The work on the muscles can be intensified still further by inhaling to lift the spine and abdomen upwards, then exhaling and stretching forwards. Aim to get your chin rather than your forehead on to the floor; this will seem a ridiculous impossibility at first, but little by little the impossible happens and the range of angles and scope of movement in your legs increase accordingly. Hold the first part of the stretch, and then the forward bend, for a few seconds, then inhale and come up. Lift your knees up to the centre gently with your hands, then stretch your legs out in front.

The next stretch rotates the hips the other way. Kneel with knees apart and feet together – try to sit on your heels. Keep your spine lifting and shoulders relaxed. You will feel the stretch in the fronts of your thighs. When this becomes easy, separate your feet a little and sit down between them, continuing to keep the upper body lifting and poised. When that becomes comfortable, try bringing your knees together, still sitting on the floor between your heels.

Further extensions can be explored by separating the knees, tucking one foot further round behind, and extending the other leg in front (into a hurdling position). On an exhalation, stretch forwards along the straight leg and hold for a few seconds, breathing steadily. Breathing in, lift your head and come up. On another exhalation, try stretching down towards the bent knee; hold for a few seconds, breathing steadily, then inhale and come up. Change, and work with equal concentration on the other side.

Further work can be done in this area by stretching forwards over straight legs extended out in front in a sitting position.

Working towards a front splits stretch, bend the right knee, stretch the left leg out behind and place your hands on the floor on either side of the right foot. Gently bounce,

Assisted stretching.

turning the back foot from the ball of the foot to the side and back again a few times. Then change legs and repeat on the other side.

Return to the right-leg-forward, left-leg-back position and gently ease the front leg out straight, but do not force or over-stretch. If you feel there is enough flexibility there, exhale and stretch forwards along the front leg. When you come out of this stretch, pull the front leg back slowly and allow it to relax, then change sides and repeat on the other side with equal concentration.

Working with a partner you can assist one another in a similar strong stretch, but be attentive to each other's needs and limits.

STAMINA

Stamina training will be included in most tae kwon do classes, but you may also want to do extra stamina training outside the class.

For example, a typical class often starts with a few

minutes' running around the training hall, this initial warm-up run often being varied by using different footwork (side to side, crossing feet in front and behind, running backwards, and so forth), and by introducing fast sprints. Press-ups, sit-ups and squat thrusts are also included in most training sessions, all this being sufficient to raise a sweat and lift the pulse to a good training rate.

To work out your own training pulse rate, subtract your age from 220; this number should be thought of as your maximum heart rate. Your optimum training range is then 70–80 per cent of this number. For instance, for a person of 30 years of age, their estimated maximum pulse rate is $220 - 30 = 190$; therefore their optimum training rate is between 133 (70 per cent of 190) and 162 (80 per cent of 190) beats per minute. In order to improve fitness, the absolute minimum needed is to raise the pulse rate into the training range for 12 minutes at least three times a week.

If you are going to run and practise press-ups, sit-ups and squat thrusts in between classes, it is useful to keep a training diary and to note down when you are feeling particularly good, so that you can relate it to your training profile at that time. Also note any times when you feel jaded and stressed, in order to see whether this correlates with over-training.

Running

Students may want to run outside classes in order to improve their fitness and endurance. You should avoid excessively long runs, though, and should always wear well-designed shoes, since the type of knee injuries and stresses caused by running in incorrect footwear are particularly worrying for practitioners of tae kwon do. It is also crucial to do warming-up stretches for the hamstrings before any extended running.

Press-ups

Doing press-ups, keep the body straight and do not allow the hips to stick up in the air; people with well-developed upper body strength will be able to come down to brush the floor with the chest. Exhale on the push up, and inhale as you lower.

If it feels too easy doing press-ups on the palms, do them on the knuckles. Further variations include putting one hand over the other in the forward centre line (this works the triceps strongly), or doing one-handed press-ups, with the feet spread wide, the working hand in the centre and the resting arm laid along the thigh. Another interesting variation is the jumping press-up; after every five or ten repetitions of the exercise the student leaps one body-width to the left, and then, after five or ten more repetitions, to the right.

Women often find press-ups extremely difficult to perform at first, and watch in dismay as male members of the class rattle off three or four dozen press-ups while they tremblingly struggle through eight or ten. However, a press-up is just a press-up, and if you do a few every day you will find it becomes easier. Exhale on the push-up and visualize strength flowing up into your arms and chest from under the ground.

> Press-ups help women build purely physical strength in an area which they don't usually have it, which, in itself, builds confidence. But much more, building the upper part of the body has to do with expressing confidence – being able to take from the world what you need and push away what you don't want. Coupled with the effects of grounding, press-ups done properly, may very well give us back that balance of power and victim-proof consciousness that we so desperately need. (*Stand Your Ground*, Kaleghl Quinn)

Sit-ups

Perform sit-ups with the knees bent and feet flat on the floor. Start lying back, with your hands linked behind your head. Visualize the abdomen pressing back into the spine and exhale as you come up. Inhale as you go back down, with control. Sit-ups are intended to work the abdominals primarily, so avoid flinging yourself up and down, and focus on your abdominal muscles, not allowing them to bulge out.

You can vary the sit-ups by twisting and turning the opposite elbow to the opposite knee as you come up, changing sides with each sit-up. Sit-ups can also be performed with the legs extended upwards, knees slightly bent and ankles crossed, while twisting sit-ups can be performed with a straight leg extended out a few inches off the floor, and a bent leg pulled into the chest to meet the opposite elbow. Always be aware that you are pressing the abdomen back towards the spine.

Squat thrusts

Begin with your hands on the floor, shoulder-width apart, your feet hip-distance apart, and your body in a squatting position. As you exhale, jump the feet back behind you until the legs are straight, then jump them forwards between the hands again.

Squat thrusts can be varied by having one foot forwards and one back, by adding a jump with arms stretched up overhead after the squatting position, or by standing up and performing front kicks with right and left legs in turn after the squatting position.

Pyramids

You can make a stamina-building sequence by devising a pyramid: ten press-ups, ten sit-ups and ten squat thrusts; followed by nine press-ups, nine sit-ups and nine squat thrusts; followed by eight press-ups, eight sit-ups, eight squat thrusts; and so forth, down to one of each.

At the end of training it is exhilarating to finish with a fast sequence of press-ups, sit-ups and squat thrusts. It feels terrific – especially when it stops.

Lower-back stretch

Sit-ups and squat thrusts can both create tension in the lower back, so follow these exercises with the lower-back stretch you used after back-bending exercises (page 17).

WEIGHT TRAINING

Students of tae kwon do may find it useful to engage in some weight training in order to firm up and tone any muscle groups which sedentary work, and modern life in general, have allowed to become lax. Women students in particular may wish to enhance their upper body strength by working with weights on the chest, shoulder and abdominal muscles.

If you do undertake this sort of training, you should always be careful to use moderate weights and moderate repetitions; this is to avoid bulking up the muscles excessively, as such muscle bulk is likely to compromise the extensive flexibility that is so essential for tae kwon do. You should also be aware of limiting the frequency of weight training so that you do not over-train and start to decrease your fitness by eroding your energy reserves.

If you do this sort of resistance training in a gym under the direction of a coach, it is important to explain to him or her your commitment to tae kwon do, and your particular needs in this respect. Otherwise you are likely to find that you are prescribed a programme that assumes that the resistance training is the sole form of physical training you are undertaking.

The overall increase in muscular power and resilience brought about by such mild resistance training will bring precision and edge to your tae kwon do work. However, you should remember that the most important kind of strength in the martial arts comes not from packed muscles but, in the final analysis, from correct and fluent control of *ki*.

WORKING WITH THE BREATH

When the voice speaks, it is Life speaking.
When the eye sees, it is Life seeing.
When the ear hears, it is Life hearing.
When the mind thinks, it is Life thinking.
And when the breath breathes, it is Life breathing.

(*Kausitaki Upanishad*, 111:1,2)

Breath is the bridge between the body and the spirit. By paying attention to your breathing you can link the two more coherently, and strengthen both the body and the spirit. Correct breathing is essential in physical tae kwon do technique, both for speed and for power. It is important to absorb sufficient oxygen to fuel sustained and vigorous muscle action, and to maintain an ability to think clearly. To focus a technique properly one needs to be able to control and manage one's breathing; in centring and meditation a steady rhythmic flow of breath assists greatly in emptying the mind and settling into a peaceful state.

Here are some basic breathing exercises that will begin to enhance your breathing awareness. When you do them, do not strain or force in any way. If you ever become dizzy, bring your breathing back to an everyday level, and next time you work on the breath, take it more lightly and do not 'try' so hard.

Abdominal breathing

Leading rather sedentary lives in a stressed society, many of us develop a habit of shallow superficial breathing, in which the abdomen is sucked in and the shoulders are lifted up on a breath in, and the abdomen relaxes and the shoulders fall on a breath out. This can come to feel 'normal', even though it is actually a very peculiar way to breathe as it only uses a fraction of the capacity of the lungs.

So try a different way of breathing. Sit cross-legged on the floor with your spine lifting, your shoulders relaxed and the back of your neck long. Rest the back of your left hand on your left knee, and place your right hand on your abdomen below the navel. Close your eyes and start to breathe a little more deeply and a little more slowly than usual. When your rhythm has settled down, start to breathe in through the nose, and out through the mouth. Don't blow the breath out; just part your lips and let the air escape.

Once your breath is flowing comfortably, become aware of your hand on your abdomen. Imagine sending the breath in down towards your hand, and bringing the out-breath up from behind your hand. As you breathe in you fill up, and so your abdomen pushes into your hand a little more. As you exhale you empty, and so your abdomen collapses back away from your hand a little. Do not distend your abdomen as you breathe in, nor suck it in as you breathe out; it is a light movement.

This is the way young children and young animals breathe. It is how our bodies want to breathe, even though the strictures and tensions of urban life can easily disturb them and prevent them from doing so.

Think of what is happening in the back of your waist, your upper back, your collar-bones, the area under your collar-bones, the sides of your chest. Try to let air move into all those places when you breathe in, and move out of all those places when you breathe out.

When your breathing has deepened and slowed, think about breathing in and out at an even pace. If it helps, visualize the air as liquid, and think of pouring it into and out of a container at an even rate. Make a slight hesitation at each change between exhaling and inhaling.

Feel how deep and satisfying the breath becomes. From time to time remember to notice what is happening to your posture, and, if necessary, sit up tall again.

After practising this abdominal breathing for a few minutes, gently move your right hand to rest on your right knee. Let your breathing return to an everyday level. If you have become very peaceful and remote, re-orientate yourself by visualizing the room around you before you slowly blink your eyes open to let in the light.

Alternate nostril breathing

This breathing exercise also deepens and slows the breath, and increases breathing awareness.

Sit with the spine upright and poised, the neck long. Cross your legs. Close your eyes and allow your breathing to become a little deeper and a little slower than usual.

Rest the back of your left hand on your left knee. Place the third finger of your right hand on the 'third eye' position, between the eyebrows and up a little. Check that you can close your right nostril with your thumb, and your left nostril with your fourth finger. Work out how to close each nostril with the minimum pressure possible. Then exhale steadily and deeply.

- Close your right nostril with your thumb and inhale through the left nostril.
- Close your left nostril with your fourth finger, release your thumb and exhale through the right nostril.
- Inhale through the right nostril.
- Close your right nostril with your thumb and exhale through the left nostril.

Continue with this cycle for a few minutes, feeling your breath deepen and slow. From time to time notice whether your spine is still lifting, and, if not, lift it. It is normal to find it much easier to breathe through one side than the other, a feeling that will ease after a few cycles of alternate nostril breathing.

When you want to stop, continue until the next exhalation on the left, then take your right hand away from your face, and rest it on your knee. Let your breathing return to an everyday level and collect your thoughts, before blinking your eyes open and letting in the light.

Alternate nostril breathing is useful for finding more scope in your breath, and also for increasing your awareness of what your breath is doing. It has a calming effect and can be used if you are suffering from insomnia or stress. If you want to learn more about breath and breathing, consult André van Lysbeth's book *Pranayama*; *prana* is the yogic name for *chi* or *ki*, so pranayama exercises are beneficial to the development of *ki*.

KI

Ki is the life energy within everything. It is not the breath itself; it is the breath which carries in the *ki*. Life-energy or *ki* is present throughout the universe, and is shared and exchanged between all living beings and all matter in the universe. The exchange of gases in the lungs during breathing is one example of the transmuting of *ki* from one state to another. This is the real meaning of the Upanishad text 'And when the breath breathes, it is Life breathing'. The quality of movement, and the harmony between breath and movement, are examples of the way in which *ki* is distributed within the body and can be directed outside the boundaries of the body. When the control of *ki* is improved, the quality of tae kwon do technique is improved.

Although it is fascinating to try to appreciate and comprehend *ki* intellectually and conceptually, the intensity and fluidity of it cannot be improved simply by mental effort. It must be felt – in the body, in the movement of the breath, in the spirit – and then allowed to improve in a non-attached manner.

Our Western philosophical split between mind and body, and our fundamental doubts about the existence of spirit, make it difficult to get over our tendency to divide our experiences between these two compartments, i.e. an experience impinges either on the mind or on the body. A Western person therefore becomes very concerned about mystique and authenticity; and of course the search for genuine *ki*, for genuine experience and growth, for a genuinely good and skilled teacher, is important.

In Eastern culture the union of the mind and body is taken for granted, however, and the idea of their interdependence seems natural. When studying Eastern disciplines, therefore, you have to work on intuition, on developing a better sensitivity to the truth of an experience, to the integrity of a person. It is all part of the discipline and the art of tae kwon do.

WORKING WITH THE VOICE

When the release of breath is combined with making sounds, *ki* is activated in another way. It is no coincidence that chanting is common to many groups looking for spiritual enlightenment, from Gregorian chant to Buddhist mantra. Singing or chanting together is an important part, too, of much sporting ritual; while within the military, training has some element of systematic shouts and cues, and rhythmic chanting or intoning is often used during training, for example in the US army.

Making repetitive, rhythmic sounds has a number of functions. At the physical level it improves the completeness, depth and quality of the breathing, aids the tone of the abdominal muscles and helps relax the shoulders, throat and face. The voice itself becomes far more vibrant and powerful. Becoming aware of sound vibration in the hips, chest, throat and head increases sensitivity and responsiveness in those areas. At a psychological level, singing or chanting together gives any group a sense of union and identity; this raises any feeling of confidence, courage and an inter-dependent trust. Finally, at a spiritual level there is an effect that is linked with the meditative process; sound, repeated until there is no need to make a conscious effort to remember what sound is being made, stills the restlessness of the mind and then frees it to float towards a meditative state.

Many of us in the West are deeply embarrassed about singing or chanting. The collapse of collective worship, in the white Protestant community at least, means that joining in a few Christmas carols is probably the closest many of us come to singing together for religious reasons. Singing or chanting on sporting occasions, though not always of an uplifting kind, is more likely to be part of our lives, and sometimes these sounds genuinely are positive and inspiring.

We can work on the voice in a number of ways. Let us look here at basic chanting, and then at the meaning and function of *kiup*.

Basic chanting

Sitting with the spine lifting well, and with the legs crossed (or, if you are supple enough, in the lotus position, with each foot up on the opposite thigh – see page 40), close your eyes and steady your breathing. When your breathing has settled into a steady rhythm start to hum with an 'mm' sound on the breath out. Pick any note, start quietly, and allow the sound to grow louder if you want it to. Be aware of the sound resonating in your skull.

Your breath will probably extend. Let the sound come out evenly. Feelings of self-consciousness, even when working in a group, soon evaporate as you become absorbed in concentrating on the sound, the experience of making the sound and the physical feel of it.

After a minute or two repeat the whole thing using, instead, the sound 'ee'. Feel the throat, neck, shoulders, face and head vibrating with the sound. After some repetitions of 'ee' also try out 'ah' and 'oh'; 'ah' fills the chest, as well as the neck and skull, with vibrating sound, while 'oh' makes a sound that will fill the hips too. Experiment with changing from one sound to another, and notice where in your body you sense the sound and where you feel most alive with each sound.

The place activated by the chanted 'oh' sound – the lower abdomen, three-finger-breadths below the navel (the same as the place one breathes 'towards' in abdominal breathing) – is the energy centre from which all power in technique comes. It is called *tan-tien* in t'ai chi, *tanden* in karate and kyudo, and *danjun* in tae kwon do, and it is crucial gradually to learn to tune in to this energy centre.

If you feel dizzy when you are chanting, then you are hyperventilating. Cup your hands over your mouth and nose, and inhale and exhale gently; rebreathing some of your own carbon dioxide-rich exhaled breath will soon rebalance the gases in your system.

When you want to finish, sit quietly for a few moments and let your breathing come back to an everyday level. If you have become very involved with what you were doing, think briefly about the room around you in order to reorientate yourself, before you blink your eyes open to let in the light.

Kiup

Tae kwon do techniques are frequently practised with a *kiup*, a yell made simultaneously with the technique. As the technique is executed, the abdomen contracts to push out the breath and to make the *ki*, the energy, flow out from the centre of the body and empower the technique. And the power and focus can be increased by allowing the outbreath to form into a shout; this is the *kiup*, and it signifies full commitment of body and spirit to that particular technique.

Kiup is often used in training drill to mark and focus each kick, strike or block, so that each is a distinct effort at a perfect technique, and not a series of movements that can all too easily become blurred or ineffective. When you are training, *kiup* is also useful for keeping your momentum and accuracy up when you are becoming tired. At a more mundane level, *kiup* also reminds you to breathe.

In sparring, *kiup* is used to give extra force and focus to techniques, and also as a force in itself. A good focused *kiup* can really move an opponent back or momentarily stop him or her in their tracks. An unexpected *kiup* may have a further advantage in breaking up a sparring rhythm that has become predictable, making space for an effective technique.

3
WORKING WITH THE SPIRIT

ATTITUDE

The five tenets of tae kwon do are:

- Courtesy.
- Integrity.
- Perseverance.
- Self-control.
- Indomitable spirit.

Courtesy

Courtesy should be apparent the moment you enter the *dojang*. You bow at the door in order to mark the fact that you are moving into a different kind of space, a space where the art of tae kwon do and its principles are paramount, where attention to your own and others' bodies, and safety, are constantly an object of concentration. Junior grades respect senior grades and obey their instructions immediately and without question, but senior grades also have a responsibility to respect junior grades; to set as good an example in style, technique and attitude as possible.

Courtesy is also important while sparring; the more senior student should spar in such a way as to stretch the junior student and challenge him or her into exploring his or her technique further, but not to bully or intimidate the junior student. This is quite a fine line to tread, and finding it is all to do with courtesy.

Students bow to the instructor at the beginning of the session, and to the instructor and the senior grades at the end of the session. Students also bow to one another when handing any equipment (kick pads, safety equipment, etc.) to each other, and at the beginning and end of prearranged technical sparring or free sparring. Each bow represents a collecting of one's thoughts; a recognition and acknowledgment of one's own and the other person's strength and vulnerability; a focusing on the importance of achieving the most accurate possible techniques. As one leaves the *dojang* one bows again, to close the circle of that particular session, of that particular experience.

Control of facial expression and tone of voice, and the whole Western internalized habit of competitiveness, of self-validation through arrogance, has to be reviewed in the light of the martial system of courtesy. This is not achieved all in a moment, nor does much of it happen, except intermittently, through conscious analysis. It happens slowly as the weekly repetition of the forms of courtesy filter down into an internal reorganization of values that eventually has a profound effect on one's life.

Integrity

Integrity follows on naturally from courtesy. Courtesy might begin as empty formalism, but eventually it has to become real. Similarly, the physical and emotional moves of tae kwon do are so demanding that there is little space for pretence, little energy to spare for dissembling, within the class itself. Gradually the challenges met in class start to reflect the challenges encountered outside class, so that the two eventually connect. Integrity must therefore mean carrying the whole-hearted commitment to accuracy, effort and respect into all parts of your life. It is not easy, but in the end it has to be done, or at least attempted.

The zen philosophical basis for this is the idea of undividedness:

> Two means the dualistic world. For instance, when you want to swim, there is the ocean and there is you. It is dualistic. 'Culminating in not-two', means jump into the ocean. Ocean and you become one. That is the ultimate state of becoming one. In other words, oneness is not an idea of oneness. The oneness of the ocean and you is

> something active, something that leaves no trace of form ... Being right in the midst of activity there is no form. All you have to do is just be there. This is oneness. (*Returning to Silence*, Dainin Katagiri)

Integrity is 'just being there,' when all is said and done. The hard physical training, the mental and psychological challenges of tae kwon do, create a structure within which one may sometimes manage to 'just be there'.

Perseverance

Perseverance is needed all the time: whether it is to work hard on a technique that you find difficult, or to go on working in an alive way on a technique that you find easy; to find the patience to allow an injury adequate time to heal properly, or the courage to rehabilitate and retrain the body after injury or after a gap in training; to weather any difficulties with other members of the class, and to continue to give tae kwon do priority among other commitments.

In our culture we need to relearn the quality of perseverance. Our forebears had no option; they had to persevere to survive. We have a choice; if we want to, we can live both physically and mentally at an entirely superficial level. Consider George Leonard's comments in *Aikido and the New Warrior*:

> The problem is, there is simply no tradition in American culture for a long term, strenuous practice that offers no specific payoff, no guaranteed progress. Our best minds conspire to make everything painless, quick and easy – 'Enlightenment in Ten Easy Lessons'. Rewards are constantly dangled before our eyes: If you do *this* you'll get *that.* Even educational television programs strive desperately to be entertaining, diverting. If the audience is bored for as long as four seconds, for God's sake, *do something.* After doing everything in our power to create short attention spans in children, we test them and conclude that, yes, children have short attention spans.

This is equally true in the UK, and probably in most other industrialized modern cultures. Learning the meaning of perseverance can help to free us from the chronic restlessness and dissatisfaction of the consumer age.

Self-control

Self-control is clearly a requirement when head-high kicks are being thrown around the *dojang* in an energetic manner; for a mistake in judgment could mean injury, or, at its nightmarish worst, fatality. The student therefore learns that his or her sparring partner's well-being is in his or her own hands (and feet).

Self-control is thus about truly understanding that you hold another person's body in your trust, and is one reason why apparently violent techniques have a peaceful implication. In addition, self-control is essential in attempting to follow the tenets of courtesy, integrity and perseverance.

Indomitable spirit

Indomitable spirit means an inner decision not to be defeated by any difficulty, however crushing. Tae kwon do comes from Korea, a small country repeatedly invaded, counter-invaded and used as a battleground by larger powers. Such a divided and assailed territory must often have survived in spirit only, and that spirit had to be unassailable.

Indomitable spirit will of course mean different things at different times in an individual's life. In bleak and unhappy times the courage to continue, simply to go on putting one foot in front of the other, is indomitable spirit enough. In happier and more expansive periods a broader vision may be involved. Like all the other tenets, it is useful to keep the idea of indomitable spirit in mind, and notice its relevance and implications in both training and everyday life.

MEDITATION

At first glance it may seem that meditation is an esoteric optional extra that has little to do with the exuberant energy of tae kwon do. However, if one considers the balancing of yang and yin, the masculine/feminine, positive/negative, light/dark opposites, which, in constant interaction, produce all the ebb and flow, all the current and activity of the world, it is immediately clear that dynamic physical action needs balancing with access to the still centre of meditation. Furthermore, as in the yin/yang symbol, in each quality is the seed of its opposite. In the centre of dynamic tae kwon do practised by a true adept is a feeling of stillness. In the centre of true meditation is a release of dynamic energy.

Looked at in this way, meditation is thus a very ordinary and sensible thing to do – it is not complicated or weird. It is simply a rather unfamiliar way for a Westerner to behave. Our culture is at least ambivalent about, and perhaps actually afraid of, letting the intellect have intervals of ceasing to operate; to call someone 'empty-headed', which would seem to describe the act of meditation, is far from being a compliment. We place a very high value on individual identity, and on the kind of work done by conscious effort. When the mind is empty and clear, the aspect of individual identity that we would normally characterize as personality disappears, and the work and changes that happen occur without what we would normally call effort. This may be a disconcerting prospect to anyone whose mind is trained in a Western Cartesian way. It is, however, refreshing and enlightening to meditate, and provides the sweat, effort and thinking side of training with its equal and opposite balance.

But if the superficial and self-conscious 'personality' is set aside what are we left with? The answer is that the deeper self becomes accessible. An analogy that is often used is that of a lake – the water of the lake is the conscious mind, the bed of the lake is the true or deeper self. Zen instructors illuminate the process of meditation

The lotus position.

with anecdotes and paradoxical epigrams called *koans*. These may seem empty, confusing or irrelevant, and often cannot be explained or unpacked in words. But on reflection they may open a new door of understanding. Here is a zen anecdote that reveals one aspect of the nature of meditation:

> A student once asked Joshu: 'If I haven't anything in my mind, what shall I do?'
> Joshu replied: 'Throw it out!'
> 'But if I haven't anything, how can I throw it out?' continued the questioner.
> 'Well,' said Joshu, 'then carry it out!'

Zen *koans* and stories may open the door to enlightenment, as may meditation, or enlightenment can occur spontaneously. But its experience is difficult to put into words. It is sometimes likened to the change that happens when we look at an empty glass; we perceive the space inside and the space outside the glass as different, but if the glass breaks all the space is the same. If we are enlightened the glass of our individuality breaks and we are at one with everything else in the universe. The sensation is 'empty and marvellous'.

How much a student of tae kwon do chooses to read

around the subject, or meditate, or be consciously aware of such matters, is a matter both of the emphasis placed on such matters by the particular instructor, and of their own individual choice. But whether or not it is intended or looked for, the practice of tae kwon do will lead the student into a process of spiritual change.

THE TAO

> The martial arts without the Tao are like the face without the eyes. In other words, unless the martial arts participate in the Tao they become nothing but a collection of techniques more or less organised around certain rules of physical movement.

This point is made by Sang Kyn Shim (*Tae Kwon Do Times*, September 1990), who later in the same piece goes on to explain:

> Within the framework of the martial arts, man is regarded as both a physical and a spiritual entity, as well as a member of society. Through the practice of the martial arts he is able to improve his mind and his body through disciplined action. And these highly-refined physical techniques and cultivated minds are applied to the welfare of society.

The holistic nature of Tao is well-illustrated in these remarks. Its elusive quality is notorious; Lao Tsu's *Tao Te Ching* begins 'The Tao that can be told is not the eternal Tao.' So how are we to describe, communicate, or share it?

The *Tao Te Ching* is a book written in the fifth century BC, Heider's helpful translation of the title being 'The Book (*Ching*) of How (*Tao*) Things Happen, or Work (*Te*)'. Lao Tsu, the author of the work, was the keeper of the imperial archives at Loyang in Honan Province in China. Legend has it that he had intended to ride out one day into the desert to die, so discouraged was he by the idiotic behaviour of human beings, but that the gatekeeper persuaded him to write down his teachings for posterity.

The theme of the *Tao Te Ching* is the flow of actions and energies, the question of why things work when they work, why things don't work when they don't, how the ebb and flow of opposites creates the universe. But the meaning is not accessible by direct study and analysis so much as by familiarization and reflection. If you read it often, without trying to understand it intellectually, a word, a phrase, an image, will from time to time sing out a perception that is enlightening and useful.

> Just do what needs to be done
> Never take advantage of power.
>
> Achieve results,
> But never glory in them.
> Achieve results,
> But never boast.
> Achieve results,
> But never be proud.
> Achieve results,
> Because this is the natural way.
> Achieve results,
> But not through violence.
>
> Force is followed by loss of strength.
> This is not the way of Tao.

(*Tao Te Ching* 30)

4
THE ROOTS OF TAE KWON DO

To try to understand the history of tae kwon do, we need first of all to look at the history of its country of origin, Korea.

KOREAN HISTORY

Korea is a peninsula, the gateway from the Pacific to the great land expanses of the plains of China. Furthermore, it is only divided from Japan by a narrow strip of water. Its territories are therefore pivotal both to the control of the Pacific and to access to the huge land territories of Asia.

Because of this geographical position, Korea has for its entire history been a battleground for other powers pressing in from the north and the south (or, ideologically speaking in this century, the west and the east). As has been the case with Poland in Europe, army after foreign army has invaded, counter-invaded and fought its own, not Korea's, battles on Korean soil. Furthermore, Korea has often been divided internally by its own political and territorial schisms; since 1953, for example, it has been bisected along the 38th parallel, for reasons to do with larger players on the international stage rather than to do with Korea itself.

The history of Korea is thus one of devastation, exhaustion and fragmentation, but, most of all, of survival.

Early history

Neolithic peoples migrated from central Asia to the Korean peninsula in about 4000 BC. They arrived in two groups, one of which settled in the north and around

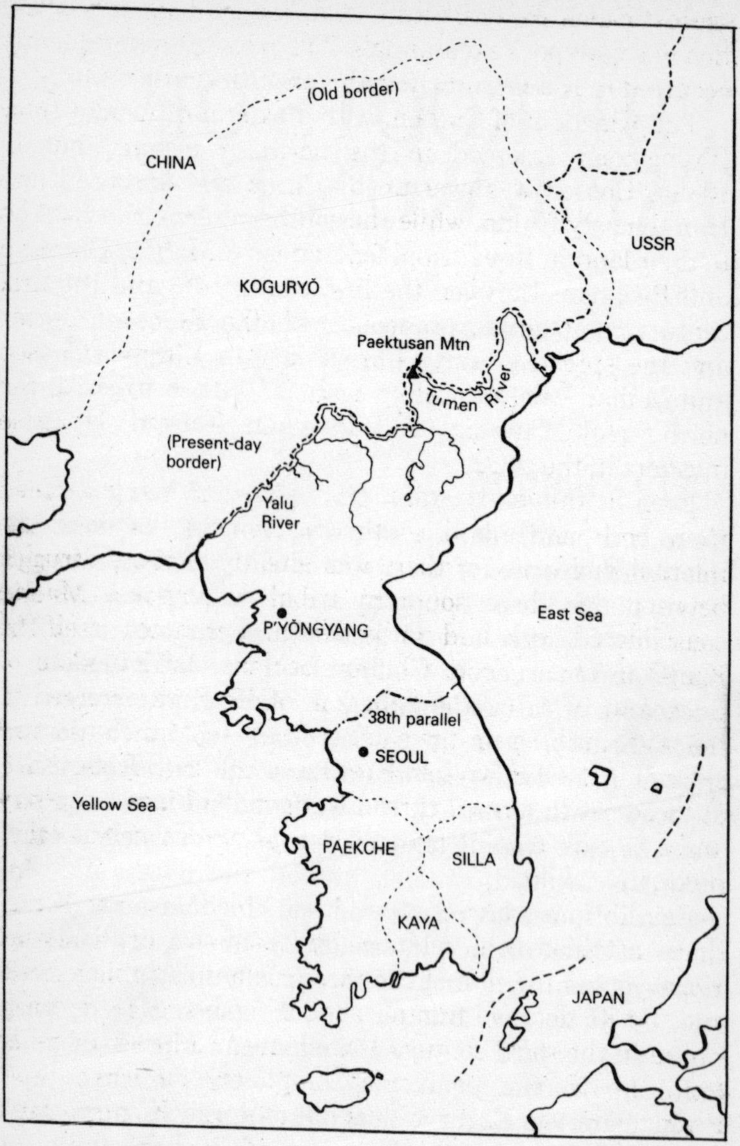

Mount Paektu, while the others crossed the Tumen River and spread down the west coast into the south. The Bronze Age overtook Korea around 1000 BC, and resulted in not just the production of bronze, but also in a growing sophistication in agriculture and the gradual domestication of some species of animals. The Iron Age subsequently occurred in Korea in the fourth and fifth centuries BC.

The Kingdom of Choson, with a capital in Asadat (now P'yŏngyang) emerged in the northern regions, but in 108 BC Choson was overrun by China and absorbed into Han dynasty China, while the southern territories held on to their land in three tribal federations – Mahan, Chinhan and Pyonhan. Between the first century BC and the first century AD (contemporaneous with the Rome of Caesar and the spread of early Christianity in Europe) Choson and Mahan were struggling against Chinese tribes in the north, while Chinhan and Pyonhan resisted Japanese invaders in the south.

Even at this early stage, the pattern of being assailed from both north and south was evident, as were the internal divisions, for there was already a power struggle between the three southern tribal federations. Mahan consolidated itself and its borders and renamed itself the Kingdom of Paekche; Chuhun became the Kingdom of Silla; and in 37 BC the Kingdom of Koguryŏ emerged in the north, taking up the southern part of Manchuria and extending itself down into Korea over the Yalu River. Each of these newly formed three kingdoms had iron weaponry and a fast-developing agricultural system, as well as other productive skills.

Equilibrium between the three kingdoms was sometimes attained, but relations regularly became volatile. Koguryŏ was the first of the three really to establish itself, and, by its decisive frontier actions against Han dynasty China in the third century AD, removed Chinese influence from the Korean peninsula completely for some time. P'yŏngyang was Koguryŏ's capital city, and Koguryo itself began to pressurize the Kingdom of Paekche from the north. Paekche, in its turn, remained an aggressive tribal unit, being in possession of the fertile lower region of the Han River – a significant area in a country which, while not radically subfertile, is without large fertile plains on which to grow food for its population (only about 20 per cent of Korea's land is arable). United Mahan groups constituting the Paekche kingdom reached the height of their powers in the fourth century AD, but then the growth of Koguryŏ began to threaten them, to the extent that Paekche tried to negotiate an alliance with the southerly kingdom of Silla.

The Kaya states on the southern tip of the peninsula never really managed to unite themselves into a proper fighting force. Silla, on the other hand, was an important and strong force by the fifth century AD; it took over Kaya, allied itself with Paekche and checked the southwards expansionist policies of Koguryŏ. Koguryŏ had already taken the fertile Han basin, but Silla and its allies subsequently retook it for their own use.

Thus, by the sixth century AD, at the same time as the great migration of German peoples in Europe, three nation states had emerged in Korea – Silla, Paekche and Koguryŏ. The northern kingdom of Koguryŏ was regularly pressurized by Sui dynasty China; indeed the Sui dynasty poured so much of its resources into this fruitless struggle against Koguryŏ that the dynasty itself collapsed in 618 AD, although the T'ang dynasty which followed also had a highly aggressive policy towards Koguryŏ.

All three Korean nation states had central bureaucratic administrations, but Silla had, in addition, the elite troops of the *hwarang-do*, an important element in the tradition and spiritual history of tae kwon do. *Hwarang* means something like 'the flower of youth', implying the best of youth, the distillation of the best of it. The *hwarang-do* reached their zenith in the seventh century AD, and the presence of these crack troops contributed greatly to national development and morale in Silla.

Confucianism travelled south into Korea in the first century AD, and became an integral part of the thought and culture. Buddhism later arrived in Koguryŏ from China in 372 AD, was introduced to Paekche in 384 by an Indian monk, and was eventually taken to Silla by a monk originating from Koguryŏ in 527 AD, Silla officially adopting it in the early sixth century. It was Buddhist religion and philosophy that became the spiritual foundation of Korea; the Buddhist culture influenced architectural and artistic expression, and led to international contacts, through which Korean culture caught up with development in other advanced civilizations. Furthermore the desire to reproduce classical Korean and Buddhist texts brought the Chinese language and script into Korea, and stimulated the development of printing; in 751 AD the Buddhist text *Tarani* was printed, using 4,745 wooden blocks.

Internal struggles continued within Korea. Koguryŏ and Paekche formed an alliance against Silla, who thereupon linked up with T'ang China, conquered Paekche in 660 and then conquered Koguryŏ in 668. However, China, having gained a foothold in Korea again, would not leave, and Silla re-aligned with Paekche and Koguryŏ to drive the Chinese out.

Silla was now able to establish territorial unity in Korea, this stability allowing the time and opportunity to effect administrative changes incorporating some elements of the T'ang system. There was an extravagant aristocracy, a large body of slave labour, and a flowering of temple art and architecture. This unity and peace lasted till the late eighth century, when power-broking amongst the aristocrats destabilized and eventually destroyed Silla, and in 935 the last king of Silla surrendered to Koryo, the new northern territorial kingdom that had been established in 918.

General Wang Kon had founded this new dynasty in 918 in the north, and had named it Koryo to symbolize the fact that it was a successor to Koguryŏ. He established an efficient central bureaucracy, based on the Chinese system, with salaried administrators, and in 958 adopted the civil service exams. A closed hereditary autocracy led Koryo, with a policy of working for national unity, and an agricultural economy. Defensive walls were constructed around the capital and a long wall was made between the mouth of the Yalu and Togury'o on the east coast.

The middle ages

From the thirteenth century onwards the Mongolian empire pressurized Koryo to sever all ties with China, and, when Koryo refused, Mongolian troops invaded repeatedly; six invasions over the next 25 years devastated the country and the population, thousands of men and women being taken as prisoners and slaves. The middle of the fourteenth century also saw further aggressors attacking Koryo, these being the nomads known as 'red turbans' coming from the north, while Japanese pirates invaded Korean territories from the south and the west.

However, the Buddhist tradition grew stronger during this period. Printing skills were also much improved; two books about the three kingdoms, *Samguk Sagi* and *Samguk Yusa*, being published in 1145. Trading with Arab traders in China not only brought cotton, gunpowder, spices, drugs and a new calendar to Korea, but also information about astronomy, geography, mathematics, book-keeping and expertise in new agricultural methods.

The Koryo dynasty was finally overthrown in 1392 by a military coup led by General Yi, who established the next dynasty. He renamed the country with its ancient name *Choson*, the land of morning calm. A new capital was established in Seoul, with inner and outer defensive walls, the city rationally designed as in ancient Rome or modern Manhattan, with a grid of streets and boulevards. An extensive public building programme created government buildings, palace buildings and ancestral shrines, their large scale reflecting the grandiose sense of self of the Yi rulers. A 28-letter alphabet called *hunmin chongum* was invented, in which the Korean language could be expressed. Systematic weather observations and records were kept for the first time. In the arts, Chinese-style landscape painting was dominant.

External contacts

Japanese incursions in the late sixteenth and early seventeenth centuries were repelled, amongst other means by armoured 'turtle' ships with which the Koreans had tremendous victories. Korea also successfully withstood attacks by the Manchus, but the costs in terms of destruction to the country and populace were tremendous.

During the fifteenth and sixteenth centuries Europeans were beginning to travel more widely in Asia, and in the mid-seventeenth century various Dutch sailors who were shipwrecked or captured were kept as prisoners by the Koreans and required to share their knowledge of Western weaponry, military tactics and ideas. One of them later escaped back to Europe and wrote a book on Korea, thus beginning the process of informing the West about Korea.

Roman Catholicism was introduced into Korea in 1608, but did not grow into a significant part of the culture until the eighteenth century, when it brought a lot of international contacts, particularly with France. Catholicism was known as 'Western learning' or *Sohak*, and was in fact opposed by the government, with specific persecutions in 1839 and 1946. The *Tonghak* (Way of Eastern learning) movement of the 1860s also opposed Catholicism, but in addition raised a voice against political corruption, the *yangban* privileged social system (a rigid caste or class system).

Tonghak proposed a fundamental philosophical position, 'God *is* man' – the same point as the Buddhist 'Atman *is* Brahman'. The point underlying this view is that the individual is part of a holy totality and therefore should have complete self-respect, complete respect for others and a peaceful confidence that there is meaning and order in existence. In the case of western religion, God or gods are often split from the self and identified as something other: eastern religion and philosophy, including the *Tonghak* movement, tend to have an inclusive and holistic feel, without a splitting between the identity 'self' and the identity 'God'.

From the nineteenth century onwards, advances in transport increased the mobility of peoples all around the world. Korea, so long isolated and occupied with internal strife and combat with China from the north and Japan from the south, was faced with the question of how it should relate to the wider world. In 1868 Japan proposed the establishment of diplomatic relations between itself and Korea. Korea was reluctant and diplomatically unskilled, and its refusal gave Japan an excuse for a hostile stance. There was aggravation, too, from the French because of the Koreans' execution of a French priest in 1866, and from the Americans, because Korea destroyed an American merchant ship in its waters in the same year. There were American and French invasions of Korea in the 1870s, and the Japanese sent warships into Korean waters to pressurize Korea into signing a treaty with them, Korea eventually acquiescing in 1876.

In 1881 Korea sent a diplomatic mission to Japan, and in 1883 to America. People returning from these missions conveyed the urgency they felt that Korea should update its systems, and how essential this would in helping to maintain national independence and identity. So it was that in 1884 a post office system was introduced which began the modernization of communications, telegraph and telephone systems following in the 1890s. A vaccination programme began in 1897, and from 1896 a Korean language newspaper called the *Independent* appeared, giving support to nationalist feelings and policies.

In 1894 the *Tonghak* sect started a revolution. Japan thought Korea would ask China for help, paving the way eventually for Russia to gain control of Korea, and therefore sent marines into Korea. China then sent troops into Korea, too, at which point Korea asked both foreign forces to withdraw. This was the first example of a new trend, in which Korea was not only invaded by alien powers, but also used as a battleground by them. On this occasion Japan won, and so had the upper hand in Korea, but the northern influence was represented by various puppets of Russia in the Korean cabinet, who were able to influence policy in ways favourable to Russian interests.

The twentieth century

In 1905 Japan finally seized Korea, annexed it in 1910 and ruled there till 1945, with a militaristic style of government curtailing freedom of the press, of speech and of assembly. The Korean language newspaper, the *Independent*, was closed down, the teaching of Korean history banned and many nationalists interned.

In 1943 Great Britain, USA and China signed the Cairo Declaration, in which it was stated that Korea should be an independent nation 'in due course'. In fact the USA planned to divide Korea along the 38th parallel, and control the south itself, with the USSR controlling the north, the 1945 Moscow agreement eventually putting this into practice in a five-year trusteeship. The Koreans, not surprisingly, were angry, insulted and bitter; their country was being used as a metaphor for the superpower struggle, and as the arena for violence that might arise from that struggle. Sure enough, on 25th June 1950, North Korean troops, trained and supplied by the Communists, invaded South Korea. The United Nations and the USA sent troops in to intervene, who resisted the North Korean army, an armistice eventually being signed on the 27th July 1953.

A series of republics then ensued in the South, punctuated by student uprisings protesting against political corruption. At the same time South Korea pushed itself extremely successfully from a primarily agricultural economy into the industrial and technical age, as evidenced in particular by a high rate of economic growth.

President Pak of the Fourth Republic was assassinated in 1979, and his place was taken by General Chun, pledged to build a 'democratic welfare society'. But political restlessness continued in Korea throughout the 1980s and into the 1990s, the goal of re-unification being beset by difficulties arising from this complex history, the continuing instability around Korea's borders and powerbroking in the east.

At the time of writing a Communist dictatorship under the leadership of Kim Il Sung prevails in the North, and a democracy, the conduct of which is constantly challenged by radical students, in the South. The collapse of the Berlin Wall and the re-unification of Germany has shown us all that the unimaginable can happen. However, for the similar barrier at the 38th parallel to come down, the North would have to be willing to take the risk of opening up its closed society to outside influences, and to considerable liberalizations in the fields of human rights and freedom of information. The South, in its turn, would have to be prepared to underwrite the huge cost of supporting the economy of North Korea while it caught up with the South's highly sophisticated industrialization. And both halves of Korea would face enormous human and political costs in order to integrate their two, by now radically different, cultures and ideologies.

The sheer success of the South Korean industrial miracle has led to a strange twist, in that it is now, as an economic success, attractive as an ally to the USSR and China, who in the early 1990s were planning an embassy and a trade mission respectively. Once again the balance of power and opportunity within Korea and the changing equilibriums that will shape its future seem to rest with the international powers who surround the country geographically or who have an ideological, military or trade-based investment in controlling its future, rather than with its own identity and will.

HISTORY OF TAE KWON DO

On the tower wall of a Buddhist temple in Kyongju, capital city of the ancient kingdom of Silla, are carved two figures in a tae kwon do stance. The temple is 2,000 years old, and gives us a time marker for the earliest known artistic record of tae kwon do. These carvings, as well as mural paintings which appear on the walls of tombs in Koguryŏ, dated to between AD 3 and AD 427 and showing men performing tae kwon do exercises, indicate that tae kwon do was evolving in Korea before the journeys of Boddidharma, dated around the sixth century AD. We know, therefore, that there was already an indigenous Korean martial art at this early stage.

In the Silla kingdom culture, contemporaneous with the

Koguryŏ tomb paintings, tae kwon do – in its earliest form known as *soo bak* (punching and butting) – was much refined and taught to the elite troops of the *hwarang*, the flower of youth. These troops, renowned for their toughness, precision and courage, in much the way that the SAS might be in the UK today, studied *soo bak*, and added to it techniques developed from observation of wild animals fighting, particularly their offensive and defensive stances.

Buddhist monks, travelling from China to found and service zen temples in Korea from the sixth century AD onwards, brought the Chinese open-hand style of *kwon bop*, and Japanese incursions brought their open-hand style, *karate*. So as time went on the *hwarang* also incorporated their favourite techniques from styles taught by the Buddhist monks, arriving at a vigorous system with body and mind working as one – *soo bak do* (the art of punching and butting) or *tae kyun* (kicking and punching). The technique of *soo bak* and the fierce warrior spirit nurtured by its practice enabled *hwarang* warriors to put to flight the Sui dynasty forces from China, even though the Chinese far outnumbered the Koreans.

Tae kwon do – still called *soo bak* at this time – flourished through the Koryo and the Yi dynasties, expertise in *soo bak* often being sufficient to ensure substantial military promotions. The Koryo period in particular was a crucial source of technique and motivation, as the population was very much preoccupied with warfare at this time. During the Yi period, in contrast, the art was used more as a route to health, fitness and personal fulfilment. However, anyone who wanted to work for a military department had to be proficient in *soo bak do*, for it was part of the entrance requirement; and King Chongjo of the Yi dynasty published an illustrated textbook of the martial arts called *Muje-Dobotongi*, which included a prominent section on *soo bak do*.

During the Japanese occupation of Korea from 1910 to 1945 tae kwon do was outlawed, and driven underground; it could only be practised and kept alive in secret. When Korea was liberated from Japanese occupation in 1945 a number of Koreans who were interested in tae kwon do took initiatives to revive and spread the art, reflecting the desire to re-establish and re-assert a national and cultural identity. Several schools were founded by different masters, with styles differing in emphasis and interpretation. A number of different names had been given to the art between 1910 and 1950, amongst them *kong soo* (empty hand), *tang soo* (China hand), *hwarang-do* (warrior spirit) and *tae kyun* (kicking and punching), and during the 1950s and 1960s many of them formed themselves into associations – Korea Tang Soo Do Association; Korea Soo Bak Do Association; Korea Tae Soo Do Association; and Korea Tae Kwon Do Association, which was inaugurated in September 1961.

In 1972 *Kukkiwon* was built in Seoul to train advanced tae kwon do students from all over the world, and it remains a mecca to students of tae kwon do. In May 1973 the first World Tae Kwon Do championships were held at *Kukkiwon*; 30 countries participated, and the World Tae Kwon Do Federation was formed by officials representing their countries at this tournament, Dr Un Yong Kim being elected as president. Tournaments are held bi-annually, and by the 1979 WTF tournament, held in Stuttgart, Germany, 80 countries were participating. Major international championships are also held in Europe, Africa, the Middle East, South America, and all over the USA. In May 1981 the International Olympic Committee approved the inclusion of tae kwon do in the 1988 Games to be held in Seoul in South Korea.

TAE KWON DO AND KOREA TODAY

If one reads and talks with commentators on Korea today, one gets a picture of a culture of complex texture.

Ham Sok Hon, a prominent Korean Quaker, takes an inclusive view of Buddhism and Confucianism. His book *Queen of Suffering: A Spiritual History of Korea* is an attempt to find coherence and meaning in the shattering record of invasion and destruction visited on Korea. The

1985 edition and translation records in its introduction Ham Sok Hon's frequent incarcerations during his long life, both in the north and the south of the country, and his work as a farmer, a teacher and a person who has spoken out about his humanitarian vision throughout his life.

In his summary he criticises Korean culture for its lack of sensitivity and taste, brought about, he believes, by overkill in suffering: 'These people have no joy in life, they have never had the liberality of mind to relish life. Always drowsing, always scowling.' However, he sees in the suffering an opportunity, from his philosophical point of view, to grow in strength: 'It is not just that we have a history of suffering, but that, bearing the burden, we live on. We are more than death. That is true Korea.' He concludes that to the spiritual dimension of the experience, and to the courage of long endurance, must be added imaginative rational process, in order to conserve and build a better future: 'The way to national salvation is the way of intellect, although at first it seems as if the whole country will be inundated, thrown into confusion. Put down your sword and think hard.' The picture Ham Sok Hon gives us, then, is of a nation still feeling the pain of being split, still trying to come to terms with a tragic history.

P.J. O'Rourke is a journalist who characterizes himself as a 'Trouble Tourist – going to see insurrections, stupidities, political crises, civil disturbances, and other human folly'. He writes about these with ironic wit and cynical despair, but also with some clear desire to cut through propaganda, lies and other claptrap, and produce some sort of truthful record of events. O'Rourke visited Korea in 1987 to report on the student riots at the time of the presidential elections; and he found the students hostile towards him as an American, even though proper press freedom is a big issue to these students.

In *Holidays in Hell*, O'Rourke comments on the cleanliness of the streets – 'You can spend twenty minutes in an agony of embarrassment trying to figure out what to do with a cigarette butt' – and the industriousness of the poor, where, visiting a poor area he and his photographer found everyone working and productive, such that they 'felt like big, pale drones in the hive of the worker bees'. However, the phenomenon he concentrates on is the sense of group, the uniformity of action, the 'spontaneous regimentation'. Satirizing this behaviour makes his essay extremely funny, as well as grim, and carries his own point of view. He is committed to the idea that respect for the individual is crucial in any attempt at civilization:

> Western civilisation not only provides a bit of life, a pinch of liberty, and the occasional pursuance of a happiness, it's also the only thing that's ever tried to. Our civilisation is the first in history to show even the slightest concern for average, undistinguished none-too-commendable people like us.

Fair enough – thought-provoking, and true. However, any Western student of *tae kwon do* will have come up against the challenge to their thinking and identity posed by the idea of 'training as one' – the aspect of 'spontaneous regimentation' that appears in the art. Personal idiosyncrasies of style are not encouraged; patterns should be performed in synchronization; *kiups* should sound in unison (not the staccato scatter of sounds that happens when members of the class get out of step with one another). One second dan comments, 'I'm always concerned when I visit a club where people are training as individuals and not as a group – I know there's some misunderstanding of tae kwon do going on.' Our Western concern with individuality contrasts with this emphasis on learning to synchronize, on learning a precise technique, on learning to move as one, and gives the Western student a paradox on which to reflect. Perhaps it ultimately echoes the Platonic idea that only within clear structure is any real freedom possible.

It is certainly true that this formality and structured behaviour creates a calm often appreciated by tae kwon do students from the UK who go to visit *Kukkiwon*:

> Korea is called Choson – the Land of Morning Calm. I felt this calm as soon as I got off the plane in Seoul, the serenity of Korean people. Everything is very formal, for example there is a strong contrast between the filth, the noise and the violence in the London underground, and the Korean underground which is clean, calm and ordered. The organised and quiet atmosphere comes from the religious and the feudal background, both structured and regimented.
>
> *visiting 2nd dan*

The behaviour which to O'Rourke seems ludicrous, such as, 'They yell at you if you cross against a light', may seem to someone else simply to be part of a different attitude to social norms.

Visitors to Korea will observe that tae kwon do training is a basic part of Korean education; tae kwon do is part of the national curriculum, and is taught in schools from the age of five, girls training as well as boys, though they can drop out of training at university age. The military and the police are highly trained in tae kwon do. But in spite of this high level of martial skill, visitors from the West report feeling safer not only in Seoul but also in the mountainous country regions, after dark, than in comparable city and country areas in the West.

This of course could be seen as fulfilling the ideal of the martial arts, which is, in part at least, that the more understanding one has of how one's own energies, one's own yin and yang, balance, the less need there is for violence. This analysis may well be naive in the extreme, but all the same it may contain a thread of truth. And the same thread of truth may run through our own problems of youth violence, for consider how out of touch the average British teenager is with his or her body (unless a specialist sportsman or dancer). Perhaps this physical alienation adds to their general cynicism and disaffection?

Group responsibility and group identity are also visible in South Korean consumerism, for although a Buddhist culture, the current generation is materialistic and acquisitive. Materialistic they may be, but they are very loyal to Korean brands, preferring to buy the Korean makes – Reebok and Le Caf, for example – to European or American styles. Indeed, the long-term presence on Korean soil of American troops has underlined the centuries-long Korean experience of needing to struggle to assert a discrete identity; in consumerism, as in other areas, the desire is to avoid being absorbed by western culture. Holding the 1988 Olympics was Korea's effort to throw open its doors to the world, to show the world its own indigenous culture.

Students from the UK and USA who visit Korea to train at *Kukkiwon* often find that studying tae kwon do in its own context and setting is so inspiring and informative that their own style and technique improves at a rapid rate. One student commented that 'I improved more in four weeks there than I had in four years at home.' Korea's pre-eminence in international championships is certainly clear to anyone who looks at a table of winners over the last 15 or 20 years, but it is excellence without ego; a participant in the competition at the 1988 Seoul Olympics noted how the male Korean lightweight contender won a gold with a sparkling jumping hook kick: 'and he wasn't even impressed with himself. Any British guy or American guy would be like this [making a clenched fist gesture of triumph], but he wasn't even impressed with himself. That's the true Tae Kwon Do spirit.'

5 BASIC TECHNIQUES

Basic classical technique is one of the core elements of the tae kwon do class; no matter how many thousand times you have performed a stance or a strike there is always scope to improve it.

At the beginning it is simply a matter of desperately trying to get your hands and feet to arrive in the correct places. Then, once your body is beginning to do what you ask of it in terms of positioning, you can start to bring some power into the technique. For some time this is exhilarating in itself and you hurl your limbs around, delighted with your new-found power. The next stage comes when the student notices, or has pointed out, that energy is leaking uselessly in all directions. He or she then sees that the whole technique needs tidying up and refining for months, if not years, so that there is no spillage of energy and all is concentrated at the appropriate focus for the particular technique.

Basic technique consists of stances, blocks, punches and kicks.

STANCES

Correct stance is vital; it is the foundation of the rest of the body. If the contact with the floor is wrong, the position of the pelvis and the angle of the spine will be wrong too, so it will be difficult to get poise and power into the technique. Your balance is also bound to be compromised if the distribution of weight between the feet, and indeed between the ball and heel of each foot, is misplaced in any way.

Generally, when moving from one stance to another, or stepping forwards, backwards or to the side in a stance, the spine should be kept lifting and centred above the hips. It is important to try not to lean in the direction of the technique to be used, as this clearly signals your intention to your opponent and removes some of the element of surprise.

Below are the initial basic stances. Advanced students will learn a variety of other stances in addition to these.

Attention stance, *charyot soegi*

In attention stance the feet are together and pointing forwards. The legs are straight, but the knees are not over-straightened so that too much pressure is exerted on the backs of the knees. The tailbone is tucked under and the abdomen lifted in order to lift the spine, making the body tall, the chest open and the shoulders relaxed. The back of the neck is long and the crown of the head lifts. The face is serene but alert, mouth and eyes relaxed. Arms are straight down by the sides and palms may face inwards to the thighs, or the hands may be brought to waist level in fists with elbows pointing straight backwards, then straightened briskly down to the sides as the feet are stepped together.

Bow, *kyungye*

From attention stance, bow with a straight back, arms kept into the sides. Do not keep your gaze on the person to whom you are bowing, as this would suggest that you do not trust them not to launch a surprise attack while you are bowing.

The bow is a time to collect your thoughts, to show your respect and appreciation for your teacher or your partner in sparring or a technical exercise. If you are bowing to someone you dislike, or find difficult, or do not hold in very high regard, it is a moment for self-discipline, a time to show respect for the person as a fellow-member of the human race, and to notice that their good qualities may not be instantly obvious, but are undoubtedly there nevertheless.

Ready stance, *choonbi*

The student maintains his or her gaze focused straight ahead. The feet step hip-distance apart and are parallel, toes pointing forwards. There is equal weight on each foot, and equal weight between the ball and the heel of each foot.

Inhale the breath into the abdomen, and with it inhale *ki* deep into the pelvis. Simultaneously bring the fists up over the solar plexus, elbows bent slightly out to the sides. Exhale strongly, bringing the fists down in front of your lower abdomen. Make the downwards movement of the fists last the same length of time as the exhalation, and push the last bit of breath out strongly, meanwhile placing power in the fists, feet and abdomen (see page 14 for an illustration). The stance should be strong and the fists full of power. The abdomen will also be strong. Sometimes an instructor will test this in senior students by striking them in the abdomen when they have moved into *choonbi* position.

Choonbi is the position that precedes all the *poomse* forms. It is also usually assumed before the practice of classical drill. Where *charyot* and *kyungye* mark the collection of thoughts and the observance of respect for fellow students and for the art, *choonbi* is the time to flood the body with *ki* and make energy ready to harness in technique.

Horseriding stance, *choochoom soegi*

To move into horseriding stance the student inhales and, with hands in fists, stretches the hands in front, wrists crossed, at about solar plexus level. On the exhalation, step the left foot $2\frac{1}{2}$ feet or so away from the right foot, simultaneously pulling the fists back, palm-side up, at waist level. Feet are parallel, with the toes pointing forwards, and the knees are bent into a half squat. The spine and abdomen lift, and the shoulders are relaxed.

Choochoom soegi is a very stable stance, and a strong base for attacking and defending to either side. Its stability makes it a useful stance for the practice of hand strikes and blocks.

Remaining in *choochoom soegi* for any length of time greatly strengthens the thighs. Beginning students will find their thighs aching and perhaps even shaking after some minutes in *choochoom soegi*, but persevering with it will toughen up the muscles of the thighs.

Front stance, *apkoobi*

In front stance, *apkoobi*, step one foot forwards about two shoulder-widths' distance (see page 65 for illustration). Keep the back knee straight and bend the front knee, keeping the shin vertical. The torso remains centred and upright over the hips, which face completely forwards. The weight is distributed 60 per cent on the front leg and 40 per cent on the rear leg, and the fists, fingers upwards, are ready at belt level, with the elbows bent straight backwards. The feet must be no less than shoulder-width apart, or the stance will be shaky and unstable.

Apkoobi is strong and stable as a launching pad for attacks and defences to the front, and a strong stance to which to move into and out of for practising blocks, strikes and kicks in fluid and smooth style.

Taeguek four, *sah jang*. This is move 3, students in *dwit koobi*, back stance.

Back stance, *dwit koobi*

In back stance, *dwit koobi*, the feet are one step apart. The front foot points directly forwards, and the back foot is turned at 90° to the front foot, chest and hips facing squarely in the direction of the toes of the back foot. The weight is distributed 60 per cent onto the back leg and 40 per cent onto the forward leg. Hands move into double guarding block. The student turns to look forward along the direction of the front foot.

This is a flexible stance from which kicks can be made with the front or the back foot, and which has forward, backwards and side-to-side potential and mobility. Using back stance, movement not only can be very quick; it can also be in the irregular rhythm so vital for success in free sparring. Because the torso is turned sideways on to an attacker or opponent, most of the vulnerable body targets are difficult for the opponent to reach.

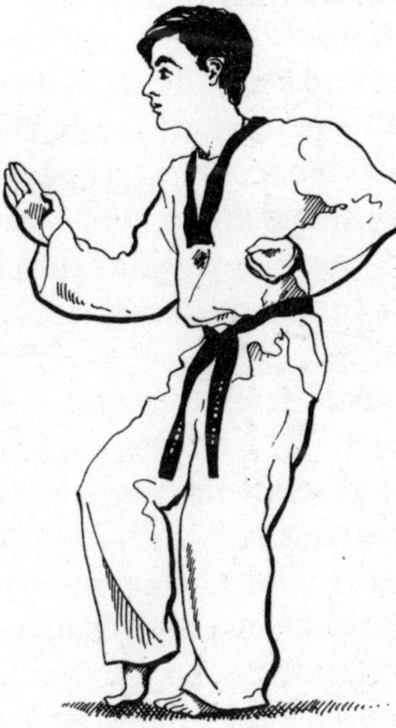

Boem soegi, cat stance.

Cat (tiger) stance, *boem soegi*

Both feet face forwards in *boem soegi*, the front foot one small step in front of the back foot, and the heel of the front foot raised one fist-distance above the floor. As much body weight as possible is on the back foot. The knees are bent and the hips lowered somewhat, although the back stays straight.

Boem soegi is useful for defensive and close-range fighting; one can kick out quickly in a limited space.

Walking stance, *apsoegi*

In walking stance both feet point forwards; as the name suggests, it is a natural stance. The steps are short ordinary-length steps, and the hips and chest face squarely forwards. The whole body is relaxed but alert.

BLOCKS

In both blocks and strikes (see page 70) Newton's third law of motion is in play. This is the law that states that 'Every action has an equal and opposite reaction.' In most block or strike techniques the action of the block or strike itself is balanced by an equal and opposite movement on the other side of the body. If this is done correctly the power of the technique is much enhanced. The push–pull pattern prevents the energy of the technique itself being dissipated by the power rippling out, as it were, through the rest of the body. To do the counter-movement properly seals the power into the technique.

A block stops a blow from an opponent or attacker connecting with oneself. Most blocks are done with the arms or hands, although some are performed with legs and feet. Blocks are learned formally, and practised constantly, the body thus learning a fluid reflex reaction to a threat.

There are many more blocks and variations than those listed below, which students go on to learn at more advanced levels. However the following core blocks are useful basics for beginning students. When practising blocks, do so moving forwards and backwards in front or back stance, *apkoobi* or *dwit koobi*, and time the movement so that the block snaps into completed position and maximum focus exactly at the moment that the step finishes.

Lower block, *arae makki*

Arae makki is used against kicks and punches aimed to the lower abdominal or groin area and is formally learned and practised initially in front stance.

In *apkoobi*, front stance, with the right foot forwards, the right fist is crossed over the chest with its palm-side near the left ear, while, simultaneously, the left arm is across the chest in the opposite direction under the right arm with the left fist palm-side towards the body at about belt level on the right side.

To perform *arae makki* one sweeps the right forearm down across the abdominal and groin areas, bringing the right fist into focus above the right thigh (in walking stance the right elbow stays more bent and the block is completed with the right fist above the lower abdomen). At the same time the left arm snaps back into a backward elbow strike, fist palm-upwards at waist level.

Arae makki, low-section block.

The whole body is full of relaxed power as the movement is performed. At the last instant, as the arms and fists finish moving with the exhalation, the fists 'snap' round into their final position. This last-instant twist adds considerably to effectiveness.

Upper block, *eolgol makki*

This block is a defence against straight punches and strikes to the face and head, and overhead attacks to the head.

In *apkoobi*, front stance, with the right foot forward, the block starts with the left fist, palm-side down, above the right shoulder, and the right fist crossed over the chest below the left elbow, as though punching to the mid-section of an opponent standing behind. The right forearm is swept up to bring it across the chest and across the face, then snapped into its final blocking position two fist-widths above and two fist-widths in front of the forehead. At the same time, the left arm sweeps back into a backward elbow strike to an opponent behind, finishing with the fist, palm-side up, at waist level.

Eolgol makki, high-section block.

Inner block, *momtong makki*

The inner block protects against attacks to the chest, ribs and solar plexus.

In *apkoobi*, front stance, with the right foot forwards, extend the left arm straight ahead to the mid-section, with the hand in a fist. Swing the right arm, elbow bent and fist facing palm forwards, out to the right side so that the fist is behind and just above the shoulder.

The blocking movement is a sweeping movement in and round to the front of the body; the fist snaps, palm inwards and arm still bent, in front of the centre of the chest. Simultaneous with this, the other fist is pulled back, palm-side up, to belt level, thus making a backward elbow strike to an opponent behind.

Outer block, *momtong bakat makki*

Momtong bakat makki protects the chest, ribs and solar plexus, just as *momtong makki* does, but it pushes the attack out to the side rather than down to the centre.

To perform *momtong bakat makki* in *apkoobi*, front stance, cross the forearms in front of the chest with both fists palm-side down, and the right blocking forearm underneath the left one. The blocking movement pulls the right forearm across the chest in a sweep, finishing with a last-second twist that snaps the fist, palm-side in, in front of, and on a level with, the shoulder. At the same time the left fist pulls back to the hip, palm-side up, at belt level, and the elbow strikes to the rear.

Knife-hand block, *sonnal makki*

The knife-hand blocks can be made at the mid-section level (protecting chest, ribs and solar plexus) as well as at a high section (protecting face or head level) or low section (protecting lower abdomen, groin and thigh). Knife-hand blocks are often formally drilled in back stance, *dwit koobi*, but it is a quick and flexible block that can be made from any stance. In a single knife-hand block the leading hand blocks and the rear hand pulls back to the hip and attacks with an elbow strike behind. In a double block the rear hand may come, palm upwards, to protect the solar plexus.

To form a knife-hand, pull the thumb in next to the fingers (if the thumb is left sticking out it can all too easily be broken or sprained). Bend all the fingers slightly at each joint, forming a shallow curve with the hand; this protects the hands. If the fingers were straight they would be at risk of breaking on impact of either block or strike technique; with the fingers curved, the hand is a better shock absorber.

The shape of the mid-section knife-hand block is as follows. In *dwit koobi*, back stance, with the right foot in front, the right forearm is across the chest, the right knife-hand is brought in with the palm next to the ear, and the left arm is across the body, with the hand in a fist, palm-side towards the body. With the familiar push–pull action–reaction movement the left arm pulls back, rear elbow strike, and the blocking hand sweeps outwards and arrives, elbow bent, with the fingertips of the knife-hand at shoulder level. The blocking surface is the outer edge of the knife-hand palm, from the base of the little finger to the wrist.

Sonnal makki, knife-hand block, can also be brought from the outside in the manner of *momtong makki*, inner block.

X-block, *otkolo makki*

Double fists form a powerful block and interception to kicks and strikes.

Some styles bring a low-section X-block from the side of the rear leg, fists pulled back at waist level, then swung down and snapped into position in front of the groin. Other styles begin with the fists, palm-sides up, pulled in at belt level, and move to a crossed position, arms straight, palm-sides of fists facing in towards the body at belt level, then twisted down to protect the groin and lower abdomen in the front centre. The fist of the leading-foot side is under the other.

High-section X-block rises to protect the head and face

Ap-chagi, front kick, blocked by low-section X-block.

from front and overhead blows. Fists start in at the waist, palm-side up, and are thrust upwards, crossed, with the leading-leg-side fist on top this time, above and in front of the forehead.

Knife-hand X-block (*sonnal otkolo makki*) can be performed with the same preparatory movement flowing into a focused block with the hands in knife-hand position.

Trying out the difference between *otkolo makki* and *sonnal otkolo makki,* you can feel that the X-block with hands in fists is tremendously solid and grounded, and useful in the face of an obstreperous barging style of attack, when you want to follow the block with a solid determined counter-attack. *Sonnal otkolo makki,* X-block in knife-hand, has a quick agile feel, for a swift evasion and a counter-attack flicked back instantaneously.

Spread block, *hechyo makki*

Spread block is used when an attacker tries to grab you by the lapels or the throat. The arms are brought up between the attacker's arms, and his grip is broken by blocking his arms out and away with your forearms. Potential energy grows in your forearms as you bring them up through the centre, then is turned into kinetic energy as you twist and snap the wrists into place, forcing the attacker's arms apart.

Practise *hechyo makki* in *apkoobi*, front stance. From the ready position at belt level the arms rise to cross in front of the chest with fists palm in. As you come to shoulder height with the fists they begin to move outwards. Twist both arms out simultaneously and, at the last minute, snap the fists out, palms forwards, to bring power to the block.

The same form of block can be made with the hands in a knife-hand position – *sonnal hechyo makki*. You can observe a similar difference in feel as between *otkolo makki* and *sonnal otkolo makki*; the fist version has a solid grounded feel, while the knife-hand version has a swift and mobile feel.

Knee block, *mooroop makki*

Turning sideways on to an opponent, raise the front knee high and turn it inwards. The knee and thigh are then protecting the lower abdomen and groin, and the front leg is ready to throw a kick whenever desired.

Checking front kick, *apchakilo makki* and checking side kick, *yop-chagi lo makki*

As an opponent approaches with a kick attack, one can check his movement with a strong kick, front or side, to his thigh, shin or foot, before he can extend the leg out into the kick.

Crescent kick block, *pyojeok chakilo makki*

Both punches and kicks can be blocked with the instep in an outer or inner crescent kicking movement.

STRIKES AND KICKS

The structure of the human body means that there are points where a strike landing will have maximum impact, and other points where much of its energy will be dissipated. It is therefore vital, when performing techniques and *poomse* (patterns or forms), to visualize clearly and specifically the area that is the target for which you are aiming. When you practise, clearly visualizing the target in this way will give real conviction and sharpness to the technique.

Furthermore, it is no good imagining striking at the target, because then the energy of the strike is all used up as it arrives. One must visualize striking through the target, so that the maximum energy in the strike is delivered into the target area. In this way, techniques become most devastating.

The body weapons in tae kwon do are these:

- The ball of the foot.
- The outer edge of the foot.
- The upper side of the instep.
- The heel.
- The fist.
- The outer edge of the hand, as in knife-hand.
- The inner edge of the hand, as in ridge-hand.
- The fingertips.
- The palm, as in palm thrust.
- The fingers, as in tiger-hand.

The power, the *ki*, in each strike, comes from the *danjun*, the power source below the navel. The breath in fills the body with *ki*, and the breath out makes the *ki* explode out from the *danjun* to focus with the body weapon that makes the strike.

Practising kicking

Always warm up properly before doing any kicking. Hamstring and groin injuries from kicking are easy to sustain and tedious to heal. Remember this whenever you train, or practise alone, or even demonstrate kicks to friends.

Practise with equal focus and concentration on both sides. It is all too easy to become expert with your 'favourite' leg, while in tae kwon do terms your other leg gets more and more illiterate.

WHERE TO STRIKE

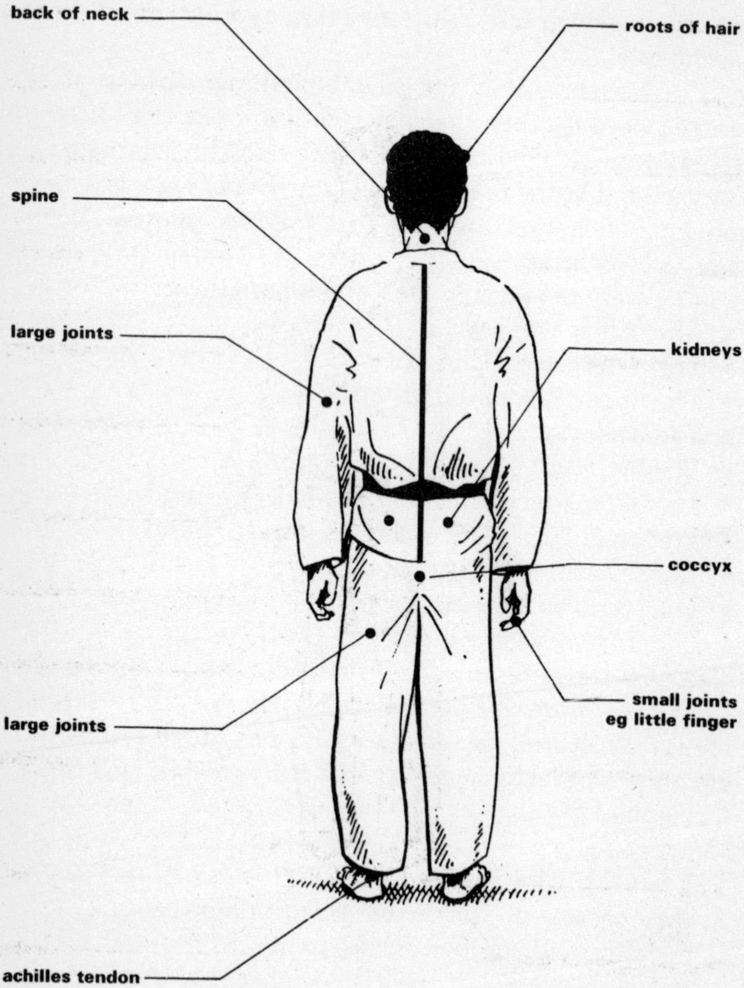

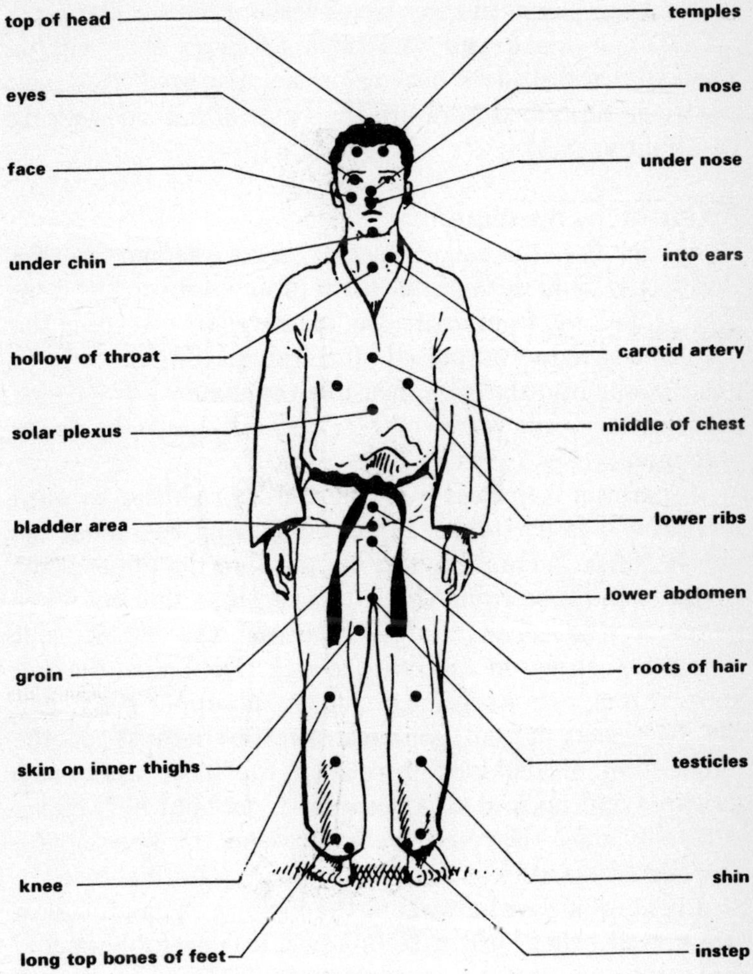

Keupso, the vital points on the body.

These kicks that follow can all be varied by performing them with a leap so that they are aimed much higher and with yet more power; by adding steps before or in between kicks to disrupt the expected rhythm; and by repeating the kick twice or even three times without pause. There are many other kicks and variations on kicks that will be learned as the student becomes more advanced. However, the kicks described here are the basis of a good working vocabulary.

Front kick, *ap-chagi*

Front kick uses the ball of the foot as the weapon, the area that focuses and delivers the blow. Momentum comes from good technique, from lifting the knee well and keeping the upper body light and poised, and from getting the hips to push power into the kick. Possible targets for a front kick are the face, the solar plexus, the ribs and the lower abdomen.

To perform *ap-chagi*, front kick, from right leg forward in *apkoobi*, front stance, inhale and bring the arms up, hands in fists, to make a flexible guard for the upper body. At the same time bring the left knee up so that the knee points at the target. Exhaling, thrust the left leg out straight, pushing the hip into the kick. The ball of the foot kicks through the target. Do not let the upper body lean too far back; it will go back a little because of the momentum of the kick, but keep the basic movement forwards and up so that you are ready for your next move. After you have delivered the kick, bend the knee again, and then drop the foot back behind you in front stance.

A neat, quick withdrawal of the kicking leg is crucial in this and all other kicking techniques. It is useful always to make time to practise the kick in four stages – knee up, kick out, knee bent, step back. In *poomse* or sparring the movement will be more fluid but will keep its proper shape if you have built those four stages clearly into your body's memory.

Side kick, *yop-chagi*

Front kick, *ap-chagi*, brings you face on towards your target. Side kick, *yop-chagi*, allows you to deliver a long-range kick without presenting your own body targets to an opponent. You can strike to the face, neck, ribs, solar plexus, abdomen and knees of an opponent with side kicks, which are often learned and practised in *choochoom soegi*, horseriding stance. The connecting surface is the outside of the foot.

Starting in *choochoom soegi*, horseriding stance, with the right leg leading and the face turned to the right, inhale and step the left foot across behind the right foot, bend the right knee and bring the right foot, sole turned slightly in towards the body, up close to the left knee, which is slightly bent. Left fist is palm-side in at belt level, right fist is palm-side in, one fist-space above the left. The body is coiled like a spring ready to let go, or loaded like a gun, at this point.

On the exhalation, pivot the left foot (standing foot) so it points backwards, while you swing the hip of the kicking leg forward and thrust the kicking foot forward, extending

Yop-chagi, side kick.

the hip and locking the knee. The arms also move simultaneously, the left fist coming in to guard the solar plexus, and the right throwing a side punch or outer hammer-fist punch parallel to the kicking leg. This has two functions. Firstly, regarding the dynamics of the movement itself, this arm movement increases the momentum of the body in the direction of the kick, and keeps the chest lifted and open in the correct position at right angles to the kick. Secondly, if a mid-section side kick connects with an opponent he will double over, bringing his head forwards in exactly the right position to bring him on to the punch.

After kicking, retract the leg quickly and neatly, bringing the sole close to the other knee, pulling the arms back to a guarding block, and then step down into *choo-choom soegi*, horseriding stance, right leg leading, as before.

As with *ap-chagi*, front kick, make time to practise the kick in four stages – knee up, thrust out, knee back, step down. Your body then learns the accurate shape of the kick, and no matter how quickly you perform it, it will keep its distinctive shape and its optimum impact.

Roundhouse *dollyo chagi*

The kicking surface with roundhouse kick is the upper surface of the instep. The kick is landed at an angle of 90° to the opponent.

Starting in *dwit koobi*, back stance, with the right leg back and arms on guarding block, inhale, open the right hip and then lift the right leg, knee bent, so that the right knee is across the front of the waist to the left side, belt level, and the right shin is parallel to the floor. As you exhale, snap the right leg out straight, delivering the blow with the top of the right instep, with the feeling of it going through its target. The right arm pulls back behind the kicking leg, increasing its momentum, and the left arm remains available to guard the solar plexus or face, whichever is necessary.

Roundhouse kick can be performed with the body more or less upright and face on to an opponent, or it can be delivered with the upper body stretching further away as in *yop-chagi*, side kick, chest facing the same way as the attacking instep.

Roundhouse kick can be aimed at face, neck, ribs, solar plexus and abdomen. It is a swift and flexible technique, very useful for sparring.

Back kick, *dwi chagi*

Back kick can be directed towards the same targets as *yop-chagi*, side kick, except for the knee, which would be a waste of the turning energy. The striking part of the foot is either the heel or the outer edge of the foot, emphasising the heel-end (where *yop-chagi*, side kick, tends to emphasise the other end of the foot edge).

Beginning in *dwit koobi*, back stance, with left foot forwards, inhale, and step your left foot a small step across in front of the body, putting the foot down with the toes pointing in the opposite direction from the stance. Gather the energy in to the body ready for kicking by bending the standing knee, bending the kicking (right) leg up, sole of the foot turned slightly in and brought close to the left knee, fists and elbows close to the body in guarding position. Turn to look over your right shoulder, keeping your eye on your target. Dip the spine forwards, away from your target/opponent, otherwise it is extremely vulnerable to any kick coming towards you.

On the exhalation, execute the kick by thrusting the hip and extending the leg, connecting with the side-edge of the foot. As with *yop-chagi*, side kick, swing that upper arm out with a side punch or side hammer-fist parallel to the kicking leg – this has the same dual function as in the case of *yop-chagi*, side kick. The left arm and fist are ready at chest level to guard either solar plexus or face and head. To finish the kick, withdraw the kicking leg quickly and neatly to the position with its foot close to the standing knee, which is slightly bent. Then step down into *dwit koobi*, back stance, now with the right foot in front. From this position you are ready to practise *dwi chagi*, back kick, with the left leg, but remember you will turn in the opposite direction.

When practising a kick that involves a turn, there is a choice as to whether to land the foot on the floor in front, or to let the momentum carry you right round so that you land with your kicking foot behind you in the original stance. As with the other kicks, learn the basic components of the kick accurately and you will always perform it well.

Dwi chagi, back kick, and its variations are a quick surprise option in sparring. One has to learn to turn fluently without making obvious preparation to do so in order to get the most advantage out of this kick. But a well-grounded back kick has a devastating effect.

Back-hook kick, *momdollyo chagi*

Momdollyo chagi, back-hook kick or spinning back kick, uses the heel of the foot to strike the target. In the spinning movement great centrifugal force is generated which makes this an extremely powerful technique.

Start in *dwit koobi*, back stance, right foot back, hands in guarding block. Step the left foot a small step across in front of the right foot, bringing the foot to the floor with the toes pointing in the opposite direction from the stance. This begins the spiral movement which winds up through the body, growing the spiral movement of the kick. Dipping the upper body down parallel to the floor, fists and elbows in to guard, lift the right leg, knee bent, thigh parallel to the ground. Look over your right shoulder and straighten your right leg, then sweep it in an arc across the target area, connecting the heel with the head or the solar plexus of the opponent. The energy of the kick is expended as the right heel comes towards the kicker's own right hip. Control the body at this point and step steadily and lightly down. Now the right foot is in front and you are ready to step across with the right foot and do back-hook kick with the left. The other option, as with *dwi chagi*, back kick, is to let the momentum of your kick take you all the way round to your original position.

Momdollyo chagi, back-hook kick, once learned, is a fluid fast technique, useful for varying pace and rhythm in sparring, and very intimidating for any opponent, since its range is long and its sweep is shocking when one is on the receiving end. Once a light balance is found in the centre of the centrifugal sweep, it is easy to recover balance after doing *momdollyo chagi*, back-hook kick, and to move into another technique.

Crescent kick, *bandal chagi*

Bandal chagi, crescent kick, can be performed in both an inner and an outer form.

For the inner form, start in *dwit koobi*, back stance, right foot back, with the hands in guarding block. On an inhalation, raise the right knee up towards the chest, shin vertical, foot towards the floor. Raise the foot up so that the leg is straight and then, exhaling, drive the foot across the centre line of the body, connecting with the sole of the foot. When the energy of the kick is exhausted, draw the kicking leg in and then step the foot down in front so that both feet are in a correct stance, ready to practise inner crescent kick with the left foot. Hands may move out at shoulder level to help balance while the kick is being executed, but come back into guarding block as the kick finishes. In the high section this kick is a useful attack to the head, whereas in the middle and low sections the kick is a good long-range block for kicks and punches.

Outer crescent kick uses the same flicking motion, arcing across the top fan of 30° or so and catching the opponent more with the outer than with the inner side of the attacking foot's sole. One prepares the kick by raising the kicking-leg knee at an angle across the body, straighening the leg up, then driving the foot across and down. Outer crescent kick has the same dual function of an attacking kick in the high section, and a defensive block in the middle and low sections.

Practising striking

Do not neglect to warm up properly before practising strikes either. Although the need to do so is less obvious than in the case of kicks, neck and shoulders in particular can all too easily be injured if the muscles are not warmed and loosened before practice begins. Do not make the mistake of practising strikes only with hand and arm power. Power or *ki* must be brought up from the *danjun* in the lower abdomen, through the torso and then into the shoulder, arm and hand for good technique.

Straight punch, *momtong jireugi*

In straightforward punching the hand is made into a fist, with the fingers curled round and the thumb tucked in, gripping over the second and third fingers. To tuck the thumb inside the curled fingers would be to risk smashing it when a punch is delivered; to leave it loosely unclenched would risk it being caught on something and damaged. The striking points are the large knuckles of the second and third fingers; those, as it were, on the back of the palm.

To learn middle punch, begin in *choochoom soegi*, horse-riding stance, fists palm-side up at belt level, elbows bent back. Practise the movement in slow motion first, starting with the left hand. Concentrate on the target, at the same height as your own solar plexus, straight ahead. As you breathe out, extend the left fist forwards towards the target, still palm-side up. At the last moment, exhale the remainder of the breath and snap the wrist palm-side down as the punch connects. This twist brings power to the punch.

Then do a slow motion punch with the right fist. As you make the right punch, simultaneously withdraw the left fist back, palm-side up, to belt level. Bring it into a back elbow strike at the same time as the front fist completes its punch. Continue with slow motion punches until the body's memory has clearly learned the shape of the punch. When you are ready to practise the punch full-speed, twist the hip, too, to add momentum to the punch.

The straight punch can also be aimed at high section, level with your own upper lip, and low section, level with your own lower abdomen.

Use the breath out to flood *ki* into the punch, and practise the punch moving forwards in *apkoobi*, front stance, punching with the same fist as the leading foot. Once you are comfortable doing this, practise moving forwards punching with the other hand, reverse punch, *momtong baro jireugi*. Even more hip power can go into reverse punch, and it is useful in sparring when you are close in to your opponent.

Knife-hand strike, *sonnal chigi*

To form a knife-hand the fingers are curled slightly but the hand is not cupped. The fingers are curved to make them more effective shock absorbers; thus a devastating strike can be performed without damage to the hand. The thumb must be kept in close to the fingers, so that it does not get sprained or broken by catching on anything. Targets for knife-hand strike are temple, neck, collar-bone, ribs and spleen.

Learn knife-hand strike by performing it first of all in slow motion in *choochoom soegi*, horseriding stance. The left arm is straight ahead, solar-plexus level, hand in a fist. The right hand in knife-hand is drawn back close to the right ear, right elbow out to the side. On the exhalation slowly swing the arm forwards, at the last moment snapping the wrist so that the knife-hand arrives palm up. Keep the elbow slightly bent, even at the complete extent of the strike – aim the strike at the neck level of someone of your own height.

Simultaneously with making the slow motion knife-hand strike with your right hand, pull the left hand in to arrive with the fist, palm-side up at the waist in backward elbow-strike position.

To do knife-hand strike with the left hand, change the right knife-hand extended in front of you to a fist, and lift up the left hand in knife-hand close to your left ear, elbow out to the side. Swing the left hand to the front in the knife-hand strike, and simultaneously pull the right fist, palm-side up, into the waist in backward elbow strike. Finish the breath and the technique at the same time.

When the movement feels clear to you, practise it up to

speed, and also practise it while travelling both forwards and backwards in *apkoobi*, front stance, and in *dwit koobi*, back stance.

Beginning students first of all need to become familiar with this strike, and then to learn the variations and different ways in which the knife-hand can be used. We have already discussed its application in blocking (see pages 67–68); but it can also be used as a strike in reverse, where the hand is drawn across the body and the torque of uncoiling it gives the strike its power. The finger-ends are the striking surface when the knife-hand is driven forwards and up into the solar plexus of an opponent, with the palm at right angles to the floor, not parallel to it.

Ridge-hand strike, *sonnal deung chigi*

To form a ridge-hand, arrange the fingers as for knife-hand, then bend the thumb and tuck the first thumb point in towards the palm. This forms a raised area consisting of the lower part of the thumb and the inner edge of the back of the palm; this is the striking surface. Ridge-hand gives a powerful strike to the temple or neck with the palm down and a movement from the outside in, or to the solar plexus, ribs or groin, moving from the inside out.

To learn palm-down ridge-hand strike, begin, as with the other strikes, in *choochoom soegi*, horseriding stance, in slow motion. The striking arm starts at the waist, hand in a fist, palm-side up. The hand doing the counter-movement starts in the same way as for punching and knife-hand strikes, straight out ahead at solar-plexus level, hand in a fist. The striking hand drives out and upwards away from the waist at an angle of 45°, forming into a ridge-hand as it goes. When the arm is almost straight it swings across and down, connecting the ridge-hand with the temple or neck of an imaginary target. At the same time the counter-balancing fist, palm-side up at waist level, pulls into backward elbow-strike position. Then the hand that has just struck is formed into a fist and held out in front to perform the counter-movement, and the ridge-hand attack is performed by the other hand.

After performing ridge-hand strikes slowly until the body has internalized the movement, one can practise up to speed, and also travelling forwards and backwards in *apkoobi* or *dwit koobi*, front or back stances.

Palm thrust, *batang-son*, and tiger-mouth hand, *a-kum-son*

Palm thrust and tiger-mouth hand both explode up from waist level, where the hand starts, palm-side up, in a fist.

In *batang-son*, palm thrust, the striking hand rises, palm-side in towards its target. As it moves it forms into the palm-thrust position with the hand held open and bent back at the wrist, the thumb in against the side of the hand, fingers and thumb curved and held away from the palm. The striking surface is the heel of the palms and is particularly effective used under the chin or under the nose. At the last second the wrist snaps the palm heel round to face the target, and the twist energizes the technique. The other hand pulls back in counter-movement as in the punches and knife-hand strikes.

In *a-kum-son*, tiger-mouth hand, the hand starts in a fist, palm-side up, at belt level. It extends up towards the target, palm facing inwards, forming itself into tiger-mouth hand. The four fingers are extended together, curved around, and the thumb is curved around opposite. As the hand arrives at the target the wrist snaps the tiger-mouth hand round to impact on it. The counter-moving arm balances the movement as before, and the breath finishes with the completed technique, as always. Tiger-mouth hand is an excellent attack to the throat.

LEARNING BASIC TECHNIQUES

Basic technique, learned slowly and methodically, teaches the vocabulary of tae kwon do to the muscles, bones and ligaments, until it is a language the body can use at will. The student gradually absorbs how each part of the body can be used in defence and counter-attack, and how techniques can flow one into another in combinations.

At first learning basic technique is totally demanding and absorbs all your interest. Then comes a phase where it seems to have become 'easy', and you long to learn and explore new, elaborate and spectacular forms, feeling fretful and restless about the time spent on basics in class. But after this a new phase arises, as the real subtlety of the basic movements begins to assert itself in your awareness. Richard Chun talks about the meaning and effects of this third phase in the introduction to his classic text on tae kwon do:

> In my own search for a meaningful existence, I entered into the study of Tae Kwon Do in the hope that it should provide me with an answer as to how to conduct my life. As I practised the techniques over the years, I came to realise that the *art* in Tae Kwon Do rested in the fact that it taught, not answers, but a way in which to explore oneself, so as to discover the correct questions. I practised movement, and learned the meaning of direction. (Richard Chun, *Tae Kwon Do*)

6
PATTERNS

> The endless succession of classes was rewarding precisely because it was, in the Zen sense, 'nothing special'. (*Aikido and the New Warrior*, George Leonard)

From the earliest stages in the study of tae kwon do, the student starts to learn basic forms and patterns – to put the techniques into coherent sequences. It is as if, having learned a number of separate words, one begins to put them together into sentences. The early basic forms and patterns are simple, although they hardly feel it at the time you first attempt to assimilate them. The sequences grow progressively in complexity until they are not just sentences but quite long paragraphs.

The practice of patterns has a number of functions. Naturally, learning the sequences helps the student to develop physical concentration. But a spiritual concentration also develops; the imagination required to construct the meaning of the pattern in one's mind, and the discipline to filter out distractions, require mental and spiritual concentration.

The patterns thus form themselves into an active meditation. Unlike the static meditation, when the body is composed and quiet so that the mind can be clear of thoughts, an active meditation provides an activity with which one can become completely absorbed, such that the mind is free of thought. Active meditation in patterns, or *poomse*, is similar to that sought in *kata* by *karateka*, in hatha yoga in the *surya namaskars* (salute to the sun) sequence, or by practitioners of the *astanga vinyasa* yoga discovered and taught by Pattabhi Jois, which is all performed in sets of dynamic sequences. In a similar way, ballet dancers sometimes experience the *barre* sequence as meditative, or even similar to prayer; I once heard a director, whose company was pioneering a new work, and who was feeling nervous and vulnerable, say, 'I feel as if I should go and do a *barre* for them or something,' just as if it was a Hail Mary or a meditative good wish. The performance of *poomse* is, then, a spiritual as well as a physical experience.

If *poomse* are practised regularly and accurately the body will of necessity become more flexible and strong, and rhythm and timing are bound to improve. Because the patterns are built up from basic techniques, those basic techniques become more and more accurate through constant repetition, and, as the student learns the more advanced *poomse*, he or she learns to combine techniques into effective fighting sequences. Moving smoothly into and out of different stances helps to develop balance and accuracy, and moving smoothly between defensive and offensive techniques develops speed and confidence. The work on imagining the assailants who are attacking you, creating the structure of the patterns, nurtures the sixth sense, the capacity for intuition.

Guidelines on how to perform *poomse* are:

- To execute each technique clearly and completely before going on to the next, i.e. to avoid running any two positions together.
- To breathe regularly through the form using deep diaphragmatic breathing, and to exhale with the last action in each position.
- To keep the fists tight and the body relaxed, except at the moment of completion of each technique, where the whole body should be focused on the action.
- To collect one's thoughts to one point in *choonbi* position at the beginning of the form, and to return to single-minded concentration in *choonbi* position again at the end of it.

TAEGUEK FORMS

Many clubs now teach the *taeguek* rather than the *palgwe* forms. *Taeguek* forms tend to be more practical fighting sequences, while the *palgwe* forms are more introspective and philosophical. Within *palgwe* there are 64 *gwes* or commands. They are grouped into the eight trigrams around the yin/yang sign on the Korean flag. *Tae* means 'bigness' and *guek* means 'eternity', so *taeguek* means something like 'the size of eternity', or 'no beginning, no end', and refers to infinity represented by this yin/yang sign in the centre of the flag.

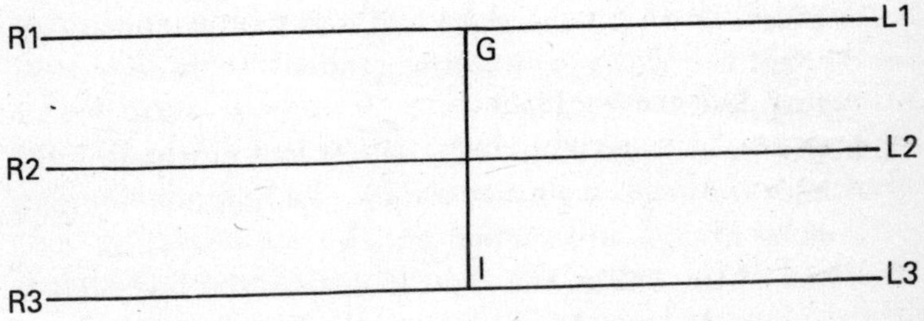

Basic floor plan for *taeguek*.

The forms of *taeguek*, which all follow the same basic floor plan, are as follows:

Taeguek one, *il jang*

This expresses the action of *keon* in eternity. *Keon* originally meant 'dry' and is identified with a dry light creativity, a masculine quality of concentrated yang energy. It is analogous with the creativity of Genesis, *fiat lux*, let there be light, as the primal creativity that brings something out of nothing.

The most basic techniques – low block, middle block, middle punch, front kick – are included in the pattern; beginning students can easily learn these, but they are used throughout the practice of tae kwon do, however advanced one becomes. Most of the pattern is carried out in walking stance, but the pattern also includes front stance, and the student learns to shift from one to the other.

The moves of *taeguek* one are as follows.

- Standing at G face I in *choonbi* stance. Collect your thoughts.

1 Turn the body to the left along the line L1. Stance *apsoegi*, walking stance. Technique *arae makki*, low-section block.
2 Step forward one step with the right foot along L1. Stance *apsoegi*, walking stance. Technique *momtong bandae jireugi*, mid-section punch.
3 Turn the body to the right, pivoting on the ball of the left foot, and step the right foot one step on to the line R1. Stance *apsoegi*, walking stance. Technique *arae makki*, low-section block.
4 Step forward one step with the left foot on the line R1. Stance *apsoegi*, walking stance. Technique *momtong bandae jireugi*, mid-section punch.
5 Pivot on the ball of the right foot, turn the body left to face I, and place the left foot on the line between G and I. Stance *apkoobi*, front stance. Technique *arae makki*, low-section block.
6 Keep feet fixed and stance the same. Technique *momtong baro jireugi*, mid-section punch, reverse hand.
7 Move the right foot to the line R2. Keep the left foot fixed. Stance *apsoegi*, walking stance. Technique *momtong an makki*, mid-section inner block, reverse hand.
8 Step left foot one step forwards on the line R2. Stance *apsoegi*, walking stance. Technique *momtong baro jireugi*, mid-section punch, reverse hand.
9 Pivot on the ball of the right foot, turn the body left and move the left foot into the line L2. Stance *apsoegi*, walking stance. Technique *momtong an makki*, mid-section inner block, reverse hand.
10 Step right foot one step forwards on the line L2. Stance *apsoegi*, walking stance. Technique *momtong baro jireugi*, mid-section punch, reverse hand.
11 Pivot on the left foot, turn the body right and move the

right foot on to the line between G and I. Stance *apkoobi*, front stance. Technique *arae makki*, low-section block.

12 Keep both feet fixed and remain in the same stance. Technique *momtong baro jireugi*, mid-section punch, reverse hand.

13 Pivoting on the right foot, move the left foot to the line L3. Stance *apsoegi*, walking stance. Technique *eolgol makki*, high-section block.

14 Do *ap-chagi*, front kick, with the right foot, then drop it on the line L3. Land in *apsoegi*, walking stance, and do *momtong bandae jireugi*, mid-section punch.

15 Pivoting on the left foot, turn the body to the right and move the right foot on to the line R3. Stance *apsoegi*, walking stance. Technique *eolgol makki*, high-section block.

16 Do *ap-chagi*, front kick, with the left foot, then drop it on the line R3. Land in *apsoegi*, walking stance, and do *momtong bandae jireugi*, mid-section punch.

17 Using the right foot as a pivot, turn the body to the right and move the left foot to the line between G and I, facing towards G. Stance *apkoobi*, front stance. Technique *arae makki*, low-section block.

18 Step right foot one step forwards towards I. Stance *apkoobi*, front stance. Technique *momtong bandae jireugi*, mid-section punch, with *kiup*.

- *Geuman*: using the ball of the right foot as a pivot, turn the body to the left and face I. Come into *choonbi* stance. Remain focused and alert.

Taeguek two, *yi jang*

Taeguek two symbolizes joy, the principle *tae*. But the character *tae* in this context is different from the *tae* in tae kwon do and the *tae* in *taeguek*. When *keon* is masculine (yang) and dry, *tae* is feminine (yin) and represents a lake – a lake bubbling with joy. The pattern should be performed calmly but joyfully.

In the pattern the student shifts from *apsoegi*, walking

stance, to *apkoobi*, forward stance, more frequently than in *taeguek* one, and *eolgol bandai jireugi*, high-section punch, is introduced as a new technique. Movement in the lower part of the body allows the student to perfect the stances, and increase the strength in the legs.

- Using the same grid as for *taeguek il jang*, stand at G facing I. Start in *choonbi* position. Collect your thoughts and focus on the quality *tae*.

1 Turn the body to the left and move the left foot one step on to the line L1. Stance *apsoegi*, walking stance. Technique *arae makki*, low-section block.
2 Step the right foot one step forwards on the line L1. Stance *apkoobi*, forward stance. Technique *momtong bandae jireugi*, mid-section punch.
3 Pivoting on the ball of the left foot, turn the body to the right and put the right foot down on the line R1. Stance *apsoegi*, walking stance. Technique *arae makki*, low-section block.
4 Step the left foot one step forward on the line R1. Stance *apkoobi*, front stance. Technique *momtong bandae jireugi*, mid-section punch.
5 Pivoting on the ball of the right foot turn your body to the left, and move the left foot on to the line between G and I. Stance *apsoegi*, walking stance. Technique *momtong an makki*, mid-section inner block, reverse hand.
6 Step your right foot one step forward on the line GI. Stance *apsoegi*, walking stance. Technique *momtong an makki*, mid-section inner block, reverse hand.
7 Pivoting on the ball of the right foot, turn and step the left foot on to the line L2. Stance *apsoegi*, walking stance. Technique *arae makki*, low-section block.
8 Do *ap-chagi*, front kick, with the right foot and drop it on the line L2. Land in *apkoobi*, front stance, then execute *eolgol bandae jireugi*, high-section punch.
9 Pivoting on the ball of the left foot, turn to the right and place the right foot on the line R2. Stance *apsoegi*, walking stance. Technique *arae makki*, low-section block.

10 Do *ap-chagi*, front kick, with the left foot and drop it on the line R2. Land in *apkoobi*, front stance, then execute *eolgol bandae jireugi*, high-section punch.
11 Pivoting on the ball of the right foot, turn to the left and put the left foot down on the line between G and I. Stance *apsoegi*, walking stance. Technique *eolgol makki*, high-section block.
12 Move the right foot one step forward along the line GI. Stance *apsoegi*, walking stance. Technique *eolgol makki*, high-section block.
13 Pivoting on the ball of the right foot, turn the body left and move the left foot to the line R3. Stance *apsoegi*, walking stance. Technique *momtong an makki*, mid-section inner block, reverse hand.
14 Turn the body left, pivoting on the ball of the left foot to face the direction L3. Do not take a step. Stance *apsoegi*, walking stance. Technique *momtong an makki*, mid-section inner block, reverse hand.
15 Keep the right foot still. Turn left to face G and put the left foot down on the line between G and I. Stance *apsoegi*, walking stance. Technique *arae makki*, low-section block.
16 Do *ap-chagi*, front kick, with the right foot, and drop it on the line between G and I. Land in *apsoegi*, walking stance. Execute *momtong baro jireugi*, mid-section reverse punch.
17 Do *ap-chagi*, front kick, with the left foot, and drop it on the line between G and I. Land in *apsoegi*, walking stance. Execute *momtong baro jireugi*, mid-section reverse punch.
18 Once more, do *ap-chagi*, front kick, with the right foot, and drop it on the line between G and I. Land in *apsoegi*, walking stance. Execute *momtong baro jireugi*, mid-section reverse punch, with *kiup*.

Taeguek three, *sam jang*

Taeguek sam jang expresses the principle *ri*. *Ri* is the south, and represents warmth and warm elements and qualities – fire, enthusiasm, hope, warmth. *Ri* is a feminine (yin) quality. *Taeguek* three contains bursts of activity linked by a continuous flow of motion, like a fire which has a central glow but also flickering flames; accordingly, it should be performed in a fiery manner.

Taeguek three gives the student the opportunity to practise and perfect combinations which are useful in free fighting, such as *ap-chagi* then *momtong doobeon jireugi*, front kick then double punch, and *ap-chagi*, *arae makki*, front kick, low-section block, *momtong baro jireugi*, reverse mid-section punch, and *hansonnal momtong bakat makki*, single knife-hand block, followed by *momtong baro jireugi*, reverse mid-section punch.

- Start in *choonbi* position, and focus on the quality *ri*.

1 Turn the body to the left and move the left foot to the line L1. Stance *apsoegi*, walking stance. Technique *arae makki*, low-section block.

2 Do *ap-chagi*, front kick, with the right foot, and drop it on the line L1. Land in *apkoobi*, front stance, and execute *momtong doobeon jireugi*, mid-section double punch, right fist first.

3 Pivoting on the ball of the left foot, turn the body to the right and move the right foot on to the line R1. Stance *apsoegi*, walking stance. Technique *arae makki*, low-section block.

4 Do *ap-chagi*, front kick, with the left foot and drop it on the line R1. Land in *apkoobi*, front stance, and execute *momtong doobeon jireugi*, mid-section double punch, left fist first.

5 Pivoting on the ball of the right foot, turn your body to the left and move the left foot on to the line between G and I. Stance *apsoegi*, walking stance. Technique *sonnal anchigi*, knife-hand strike, reverse hand.

6 Step forward one step with the right foot on the line between G and I. Stance *apsoegi*, walking stance. Technique *sonnal anchigi*, knife-hand strike, reverse hand.

7 Keeping the right foot fixed, turn to the left and step the left foot on to the line L2. Stance *dwit koobi*, back stance. Technique *hansonnal momtong bakat makki,* single knife-hand mid-section block.

8 Keeping the right foot fixed, step the left foot forwards a little into *apkoobi,* front stance. Execute *momtong baro jireugi,* mid-section reverse punch.

9 Move the left foot, then the right foot and turn the body to the right along the line R2. Stance *dwit koobi,* back stance. Technique *hansonnal momtong bakat makki,* single knife-hand mid-section block.

10 Keeping the left foot fixed, step the right foot forwards a little into *apkoobi,* front stance. Execute *momtong baro jireugi,* mid-section reverse punch.

11 Move the left foot on to the line between G and I, facing towards I, and keeping the right foot still. Stance *apsoegi,* walking stance. Technique *momtong an makki,* mid-section inner block.

12 Step the right foot one step forwards on the line between G and I. Stance *apsoegi,* walking stance. Technique *momtong an makki,* mid-section inner block.

13 Pivoting on the ball of the right foot, turn left through 270° (three-quarters of a complete turn) and step the left foot on to the line R3. Stance *apsoegi,* walking stance. Technique *arae makki,* low-section block.

14 Do *ap-chagi,* front kick, with the right foot and drop it down on to the line R3. Land in *apkoobi,* front stance, and execute *momtong doobeon jireugi,* mid-section double punch.

15 Using the ball of the left foot as a pivot, turn your body to the right and move the right foot along the line R. Stance *apkoobi,* front stance. Technique *arae makki,* low-section block.

16 Do *ap-chagi,* front kick, with the left foot, then drop it on the line L3. Land in *apkoobi,* front stance, then execute *momtong doobeon jireugi,* mid-section double punch.

17 Pivot on the ball of the right foot, turn left to face G, with the left foot on the line between G and I. Stance *apsoegi,* walking stance. Technique *arae makki* then *momtong baro jireugi*, low-section block then mid-section punch, reverse hand.

18 Step one step further with the right foot along the line between G and I. Stance *apsoegi*, walking stance. Technique *arae makki* then *momtong baro jireugi*, low-section block then mid-section punch, reverse hand.

19 Do *ap-chagi*, front kick, with your left foot and drop it on the line between G and I. Land in *apsoegi*, walking stance, then execute *arae makki* then *momtong baro jireugi*, low-section block then mid-section punch, reverse hand.

20 Do *ap-chagi*, front kick, with your right foot and drop it on the line between G and I. Land again in *apsoegi*, walking stance, and execute *arae makki* then *momtong baro jireugi*, low-section block followed by mid-section punch, reverse hand, this time with *kiup*.

- Pivot on the ball of the right foot and return to *choonbi* stance facing I. Collect your thoughts; remain focused and alert.

Taeguek four, *sah jang*

Taeguek sah jang represents thunder. It expresses the male principle *jin* of *palgwe*. Thunder and lightning evoke fear and dread, but remind us that the extreme emotions, like thunderstorms, pass eventually. The practice of *taeguek sah* helps the student to act calmly and bravely in the face of dangers, both real and imagined, knowing that they will, eventually, pass.

Taeguek sah introduces *bakat palmok makki*, outer form mid-section block, many knife-hand techniques, and two side kicks, *yop-chagi*, in combination, first right, then left. This kicking combination requires the student to improve his or her balance and coordination without losing any power. Smooth movement from *dwit koobi* to *apkoobi*, back stance to front stance (as in moves **1** to **2**), or from front kick, *ap-chagi*, back into *dwit koobi*, back stance, and then into *bakat palmok makki*, outer form block to the opposite

Taeguek four, *sah jang*, move 2.

direction (as in moves **10** to **11**), requires a refinement of the student's tae kwon do technique.

- Stand at G facing I and come into *choonbi* stance. Collect your thoughts and focus on the idea of thunder and lightning – the storm that flares up suddenly, and then calms.

1 Turn the body to the left and move the left foot one step along the line L1. Stance *dwit koobi*, back stance. Technique *sonnal momtong makki*, double knife-hand block.

2 Move the right foot one step forwards along the line L1. Stance *apkoobi*, front stance. Technique *sonkeut jireugi*, pressing block with front hand, mid-section spear-hand thrust with back hand.

3 Pivoting on the ball of the left foot, turn to the right and move the right foot to the line R1. Stance *dwit koobi*, back stance. Technique *sonnal momtong makki*, double knife-hand block.

4 Move the left foot one step forwards along the line R1.

Stance *apkoobi*, front stance. Technique *sonkeut jireugi*, pressing block with front hand, mid-section spear-hand thrust with rear hand.

5 Pivoting on the ball of the right foot, turn the body to the left and put the left foot on the line between G and I. Stance *apkoobi*, front stance. Technique *jebipoom mokchigi*, high-section knife-hand block with front hand, simultaneous high-section knife-hand strike with rear hand.

6 Do *ap-chagi*, front kick, with the right foot. Land in *apsoegi*, walking stance, and execute *momtong baro jireugi*, mid-section punch, reverse hand.

7 Do *yop-chagi*, side kick, with the left foot, landing on the line between G and I. Land in *apkoobi*, front stance.

8 As soon as the stance is secure, do *yop-chagi*, again with the right foot, and land on the line between G and I. This time land in *dwit koobi*, back stance, and do *sonnal momtong makki*, double knife-hand block.

9 Pivoting on the ball of the right foot, turn the body to the left and move the left foot to the line R2. Stance *dwit koobi*, back stance. Technique *bakat palmok makki*, mid-section outer block.

10 Keep your left foot fixed. Do *ap-chagi*, front kick, with the right foot, and pull it back to drop into its original position. Land in *dwit koobi*, back stance, and do *momtong an makki*, mid-section inner block, reverse hand.

11 Turn the body right towards L2. Stance *dwit koobi*, back stance. Technique *bakat palmok makki*, mid-section outer block.

12 Keep the right foot fixed. Do *ap-chagi*, front kick, with the left foot then pull it back to drop to its original position. Land in *dwit koobi*, back stance. Do *momtong an makki*, mid-section inner block, reverse hand.

13 Move the left foot to the line between G and I, facing towards G. Keep the right foot still. Stance *apkoobi*, front stance. Technique *jebipoom mokchigi*, high-section knife-hand block with the front hand, simultaneous high-section knife-hand strike with the rear hand.

14 Do *ap-chagi,* front kick, with the right foot, and drop it on the line between G and I. Land in *apkoobi,* front stance, and do *deung joomeok eolgol ap-chagi,* high-section back-fist strike.

15 Move the left foot to line R2 with the right foot fixed. Stance *apsoegi,* walking stance. Technique *momtong makki,* mid-section inner block.

16 Keep both feet still and do *momtong baro jireugi,* mid-section punch, reverse hand.

17 Turn the body to face the line L2. Stance *apsoegi,* walking stance. Technique *momtong makki,* mid-section inner block.

18 Keep both feet still and do *momtong baro jireugi,* mid-section punch, reverse hand.

19 Facing G, move your left foot to the line between G and I. Stance *apkoobi,* front stance. Technique *momtong makki,* mid-section inner block, then *momtong doobeon jireugi,* mid-section double punch.

20 Move the right foot one step forwards on the line between G and I. Stance *apkoobi,* front stance. Technique *momtong makki,* mid-section inner block, then *momtong doobeon jireugi,* mid-section double punch. On the final punch *kiup.*

- To finish, pivot on the ball of the right foot, turn the body to the left, and face I. Come into *choonbi* stance and remain focused, alert and still.

Taeguek* five, *oh jang

Taeguek oh jang represents the aspect *seon* of *palgwe. Seon* is female (yin), and represents the wind. Although wind can be terrible and destructive, it can also be gentle and subtle. *Seon* symbolizes gentle and good-natured actions, the effects of which can be gentle and flexible as a breeze, or powerful and unyielding as a hurricane. The form contains powerful combinations which push away resistance, then penetrate with a strike such as *mok joomeok naeryo chigi*, hammer-fist to the head, elbow strike to the face, and back-fist attacks. Kicks and blocks also appear in combinations.

- Begin at G, facing I, in *choonbi* stance. Collect your thoughts, and focus on the quality of the element of wind.

1 Turn the body left and move the left foot one step along the line L1. Stance *apkoobi*, front stance. Technique *arae makki*, low-section block.
2 Draw the left foot back to parallel stance with the right one. Sweep the left arm in a large arc back across the body, up and over into hammer-fist strike. Stance *pyeonhi soegi*, ready stance. Technique *mok joomeok naeryo chigi*, hammer-fist to top of head.
3 Pivoting on the ball of the left foot, turn the body to the right, and move the right foot along the line R1. Stance *apkoobi*, front stance. Technique *arae makki*, low-section block.
4 Pull the right foot back towards the left into parallel stance. Sweep the right arm in a large arc back across the body, up and over into hammer-fist strike. Stance *pyeonhi soegi*, ready stance. Technique *mok joomeok naeryo chigi*, hammer-fist to the top of head.
5 Move the left foot forwards on the line between G and I. Keep the right foot fixed. Stance *apkoobi*, front stance. Technique *momtong makki* then immediately *momtong an makki*, double mid-section block, left arm first.
6 Do *ap-chagi*, front kick, with the right foot and drop it on the line between G and I. Land in *apkoobi*, front stance, then do high-section back-fist strike, followed by mid-section inner block, reverse hand, *joomeok eolgol apchigi* and *momtong an makki*.
7 Do *ap-chagi*, front kick, with the left foot and drop it on the line between G and I. Land in *apkoobi*, front stance, then do *deung joomeok eolgol apchigi*, high-section back-fist strike, followed by *momtong an makki*, mid-section inner block, reverse hand.

8 Move the right foot one step forwards on the line between G and I. Stance *apkoobi*, front stance. Technique *deung joomeok apchigi*, back-fist strike. *Kiup* with the strike.

9 Pivoting on the ball of the right foot, turn the body left and move the left foot on to the line R2. Stance *dwit koobi*, back stance. Technique *hansonnal momtong bakat makki*, mid-section single knife-hand mid-section block.

10 Move the right foot one step forward on the line R2. Stance *apkoobi*, front stance. Technique *palkoop eolgol chigi*, high-section elbow strike.

11 Turn the body to the right with the left foot fixed and move the right foot to the line L3. Stance *dwit koobi*, back stance. Technique *hansonnal momtong bakat makki*, single knife-hand mid-section block.

12 Move the left foot one step forwards along the line L3. Stance *apkoobi*, front stance. Technique *palkoop eolgol chigi*, high-section elbow strike.

13 Pivoting on the ball of the right foot, turn and drop the left foot on the line between G and I, facing towards G. Stance *apkoobi*, front stance. Technique *arae makki*, low-section block, followed by *momtong an makki*, mid-section inner block, reverse hand.

14 Do *ap-chagi*, front kick, with the right foot, and drop it on the line between G and I, facing G. Land in *apkoobi*, front stance, then perform *arae makki*, low-section block, followed by *momtong an makki*, mid-section inner block, reverse hand.

15 Move the left foot to the line R2. Stance *apkoobi*, front stance. Technique *eolgol makki*, high-section block.

16 Do *yop-chagi*, side kick, with the right foot and at the same time do *deung joomeok eolgol bakat chigi*, back-fist strike to the side of the head. Land in *apkoobi*, front stance, and do *palkoop momtong pyojeok chigi*, mid-section reverse elbow strike.

17 Pivoting on the ball of the left foot, turn the body right. Move the right foot on to the line R2. Stance *apkoobi*, front stance. Technique *eolgol makki*, upper-section block.

18 Do *yop-chagi*, side kick, with the left foot and at the same time do *deung joomeok eolgol bakat chigi*, back-fist strike to the side of the head. Land in *apkoobi*, front stance, and do *palkoop momtong pyojeok chigi*, mid-section reverse elbow strike.

19 Pivoting on the ball of the right foot, turn the body left and drop the left foot on to the line between G and I. Face G. Stance *apkoobi*, front stance. Technique *arae makki*, low-section block, then *momtong an makki*, mid-section inner block, reverse hand.

20 Do *ap-chagi*, front kick, with the right foot and drop it one step forwards on the line between G and I, facing I. Land in *bal dwit koasoegi*, twisting stance, back leg against calf of leading leg, and simultaneously perform *deung joomeok eolgol apchigi*, high-section back-fist strike, with *kiup*.

- To finish, pivot on the ball of the right foot, turn the body to the left and face G. Return to *choonbi* position; remain focused and alert.

Taeguek six, *yuk jang*

Taeguek six represents the principle *gam*, which is water. Water can adapt itself to any shape or form without losing its nature; it flows and streams, and, with time, can wear away the hardest granite. *Gam* is male (yang), and symbolizes the north. Through the quality *gam* we learn that we can overcome any difficulty if we go forwards with self-confidence and persistence.

Taeguek yuk jang is flowing and gentle, but also destructive. In the form there are outer form blocks, high section, and middle and high section single knife-hand blocks, which bring fluidity and flexibility to the hips. Roundhouse or turning kick, *dollyo chagi*, is introduced as a new technique. It is followed by an immediate change of direction, which requires strength and balance in order to keep expressing the fluid quality of *gam*.

- Stand in *choonbi* stance at G, facing the direction I.

Collect your thoughts and focus on the elemental quality of water.

1 Turn the body left and move the left foot one step on the line L1. Stance *apkoobi*, front stance. Technique *arae makki*, low-section block.

2 Keep the left foot fixed. Do *ap-chagi*, front kick, with the right foot then pull it back to drop in the original place. Land in *dwit koobi*, back stance, and do *bakat palmok momtong makki*, mid-section outer block.

3 Keep the left foot fixed and turn the body to the right to face the direction R1. Stance *apkoobi*, front stance. Technique *arae makki*, low-section block.

4 With the right foot fixed, do *ap-chagi*, front kick, with the left foot and pull it back to drop in the original place. Land in *dwit koobi*, back stance, and do *bakat palmok momtong makki*, mid-section outer block.

5 Keep the right foot fixed and move the left foot one step forward on the line between G and I. Stance *apkoobi*, front stance. Technique *hansonnal eolgol bakat makki*, high-section reverse knife-hand block. The chest is turned 45° to the right.

6 Do *dollyo chagi*, turning kick, with the right foot and drop it on the line between G and I.

7 Move the left foot one step to the line L2. Stance *apkoobi*, front stance. Technique *bakat palmok eolgol makki*, high-section outer block, then *momtong baro jireugi*, mid-section punch, reverse hand.

8 Do *ap-chagi*, front kick, with the right foot and drop it on the line L2. Land in *apkoobi*, front stance, and do *momtong baro jireugi*, mid-section punch, reverse hand.

9 Pivoting on the ball of the left foot turn the body to the right and move the foot to the line R2. Stance *apkoobi*, front stance. Technique *bakat palmok eolgol makki*, high-section outer block, then *momtong baro jireugi*, mid-section punch, reverse hand.

10 Do *ap-chagi*, front kick, with the left foot and drop it on the line R2. Land in *apkoobi*, front stance, then do *momtong baro jireugi*, mid-section punch, reverse hand.

11 Pivoting on the right foot, turn the body to the left and face I, standing on the line between G and I. In ready stance, do *arae hechyo makki*, double lower block, very slowly (about five seconds). Make the exhalation last the same amount of time as the technique. When you have exhaled fully, feel strength in the feet, fists and abdomen.

12 Keep the left foot fixed, and move the right foot one step along the line between G and I, facing towards I. Stance *apkoobi*, front stance. Technique *hansonnal eolgol bakat makki*, high-section reverse knife-hand block. Turn your chest 45° to the right.

13 Do *dollyo chagi*, turning kick, with the left foot and *kiup*. Land in ready stance, feet parallel, facing R3.

14 Turning to your right, turn 180° to face L3. Step your right foot on to L3 in *apkoobi*, front stance. Technique *arae makki*, low-section block.

15 Do *ap-chagi*, front kick, with the left leg then drop it back on to the line L3 in *dwit koobi*, back stance. Do *bakat palmok momtong makki*, mid-section outer block, reverse hand.

16 Keep the right foot fixed and turn the body to the left to face the direction R3. Stance *apkoobi*, front stance. Technique *arae makki*, low-section block.

17 With the left foot fixed, do *ap-chagi*, front kick, then drop it back on to the line R3 in *dwit koobi*, back stance. Do *bakat palmok momtong makki*, mid-section outer block, reverse hand.

18 Keep the left foot fixed and move the right foot behind you on to the line between G and I, still facing I. Stance *dwit koobi*, back stance. Technique *sonnal momtong makki*, mid-section twin knife-hand block.

19 Step the left foot back one step on the line between G and I, still facing I. Stance *dwit koobi*, back stance. Technique *sonnal momtong makki*, mid-section twin knife-hand block.

20 Step the right foot back one step on the line between G and I. Stance *apkoobi.* Technique *batang son momtong makki,* mid-section palm block.

21 Keep both feet still. Do *momtong baro jireugi,* mid-section punch, reverse hand.

22 Step the left foot back one step on the line between G and I. Stance *apkoobi,* front stance. Technique *batang son momtong makki,* mid-section palm block.

23 Keep both feet still. Do *momtong baro jireugi,* mid-section punch, reverse hand.

- To finish, step the left foot forward into ready stance parallel with the right, and bring the hands into *choonbi* position. Remain focused and alert.

Taeguek seven, *chil jang*

Taeguek seven expresses the aspect *gan* of *palgwe. Gan* means 'top stop' and symbolizes a mountain. *Gan* is a male (yang) quality and reflects the mountain symbol in substance and stability. The form emphasises the skill of only moving when absolutely necessary, and of moving rapidly, then stopping solidly again. This ability to change rhythm is a useful skill in sparring.

Cat or tiger stance, *boem soegi,* is introduced, a stance that is very stable, but from which action can be quickly performed. Crescent kick, *pyojoek chagi,* is also introduced, as are several new blocks that can stop an opponent's attack without the student's own stability being threatened – palm block, scissor block, X-block and spread middle block.

- Stand at G and face I. Stand in *choonbi* stance and focus on the quality of *gan,* the stable mountain.

1 Turn to the left and step your left foot one very small step on the line L1. Stance *boem soegi,* cat stance. Technique *batang son momtong an makki,* mid-section palm block, reverse hand.

2 With the left foot fixed, do *ap-chagi,* front kick, with the right foot. Drop it back on to its original position, still in *boem soegi,* cat stance. Do *momtong an makki,* mid-section inner block.

3 Keep the left foot fixed and turn to the right. Step the right foot one very small step on the line R1. Stance *boem soegi*, cat stance. Technique *batang son momtong an makki*, mid-section palm block, reverse hand.

4 With the right foot fixed, do *ap-chagi*, front kick, with the left foot, then drop it back to its original position. Stance still *boem soegi*, cat stance. Technique *momtong an makki*, mid-section inner block.

5 Move the left foot forwards on to the line between G and I. Stance *dwit koobi*, back stance. Technique *sonnal arae makki*, low-section twin knife-hand block.

6 Move the right foot forwards one step on the line between G and I. Stance *dwit koobi*, back stance. Technique *sonnal arae makki*, low-section twin knife-hand block.

7 Move the left foot to the line L2, keeping the right foot fixed. Stance *boem soegi*, cat stance. Technique: support the right elbow with the back of the left hand, and do *batang son momtong an makki*, mid-section palm block, reverse hand.

8 Keep feet still and arms still. Do *deung joomeok apchigi*, high-section back-fist strike.

9 Turn the body to the right and face R2. Both feet stay fixed in position, but adjust to *boem soegi*, cat stance, facing R2. Technique: support the left elbow on the back of the right hand, and do *batang son momtong an makki*, mid-section palm block, reverse hand.

10 Keep the feet still and the arms still. Do *deung joomeok eolgol apchigi*, high-section back-fist strike.

11 Turn to face I and pull the left foot in next to the right. Hold the right fist within the left hand in front of you at chin level, and exhale fully, to a count of five seconds. Concentrate fully.

12 Step the left foot forwards one step on to the line between G and I. Stance *apkoobi*, front stance. Technique *bandae gawi makki*, then *oreum gawi makki* in quick succession, scissors block twice, left arm uppermost first, then right arm uppermost.

13 Step the right foot one step forwards on the line

between G and I. Stance *apkoobi*, front stance. Technique *bandae gawi makki* and *oreum gawi makki* in quick succession, scissors block twice, right arm uppermost first, then left arm uppermost.

14 Pivoting on the ball of the right foot, turn the body to the left and move the left foot along the line L3. Stance *apkoobi*, front stance. Technique *bakat palmok hechyo makki*, high-section twin outer block, then *a-kum-son chagi*, double tiger-mouth strike.

15 Move quickly one step forward on the line R3 into *dwit koasoegi*, twisting stance. Do *moorop chigi*, right knee strike pulling both hands down, then *joomeok momtong jeochyo jireugi*, twin upset punch.

16 Keep the right foot fixed and step the left foot back, forming *apkoobi*, front stance. Technique *otkolo makki*, low-section forearm X-block.

17 Pivoting on the ball of the left foot, turn the body to the right. In *apkoobi*, front stance, do *bakat palmok hechyo makki*, high-section twin outer block, then *a-kum-son chagi*, double tiger-mouth strike.

18 Do *moorop chigi*, knee strike, with the left knee, pulling both hands down. Land in *dwit koasoegi*, twisting stance, and do *joomeok momtong jeochyo jireugi*, twin upset punch.

19 Keep the left foot fixed and pull the right foot backwards to form *apkoobi*, front stance. Technique *otkolo makki*, low-section X-block.

20 Move the left foot on to the line between G and I, facing G. Stance *apsoegi*, walking stance. Technique *deung joomeok eolgol apchigi*, high-section back-fist strike.

21 Open the palm of the left hand and do *pyojeok chagi*, inner crescent kick, striking the hand. Land in *choochoom soegi*, horseriding stance.

22 Pull the left foot forwards into *apsoegi*, walking stance. Technique *deung joomeok eolgol apchigi*, high-section back-fist strike.

23 Open the right palm and do *pyojeok chagi*, inner crescent kick, striking the hand. Land in *choochoom soegi*, horseriding stance.

24 Both feet remain still. Do *hansonnal momtong yop makki*, mid-section single knife-hand block.

25 Move the right foot one step forward on the line between G and I. Stance *choochoom soegi*, horseriding stance. Technique *joomeok yop jireugi*, side lunge punch, with *kiup*.

- To finish, pivot on the ball of the right foot, turn the body to the left, and face I. Stand in *choonbi* stance and stay focused and alert.

Taeguek eight, *pal jang*

Taeguek pal jang symbolizes *gon*, which is the earth. The earth is female (yin), receptive and heavy, nurturing, silent and strong. *Pal jang* consolidates the student's knowledge, making him or her ready to move on to the higher forms; all the basic elements of tae kwon do are included here.

- Stand at G facing I in *choonbi* position. Collect your thoughts and focus on the qualities of *gon*, the earth.

1 Move the left foot one step forwards on the line between G and I. Stance *dwit koobi*, back stance. Technique *bakat momtong palmok geodeuro makki*, guarding block. Move the front foot into *apkoobi*, front stance. Do *momtong baro jireugi*, mid-section punch, reverse hand.

2 Do *doobaldangsang ap-chagi*, front kick, then jumping front kick. Land in *apkoobi*, front stance, and do *momtong makki*, mid-section inner block, followed by *momtong doobeon jireugi*, mid-section double punch.

3 Move the right foot one step forwards on the line between G and I. Stance *apkoobi*, front stance. Technique *momtong baro jireugi*, mid-section reverse punch.

4 Pivoting on the ball of the right foot, turn the body left and move the left foot to the line R1, looking towards R1. Stance *apkoobi*, front stance. Technique *oesanteul makki*, mountain block.

5 Turn the body to the left, without moving the feet. Form *apkoobi*, front stance, then do *joomeok dangyo teok jireugi*, slow upper cut.

Oesanteul makki, mountain block.

6 Move the left foot to the line of L2, step across then step the right foot one step on L2. Form *apkoobi*, front stance. Technique *oesanteul makki*, mountain block.
7 Turn the body right without moving the feet. Form *apkoobi*, front stance, then do *joomeok dangyo teok jireugi*, slow upper cut.
8 Pivoting on the ball of the left foot, turn the body left and move the right foot back on to the line between G and I. Stance *dwit koobi*, back stance. Technique *sonnal momtong makki*, mid-section twin knife-hand block.
9 Push the left foot forwards into *apkoobi*, front stance. Technique *momtong baro jireugi*, mid-section punch, reverse hand.
10 Do *ap-chagi*, front kick, with the right foot, then pull it back to drop on the original place. Step the left foot back one step. Pull the right foot back into *boem soegi*, cat stance. Do *batang son momtong makki*, mid-section palm block.
11 Move the left foot on to the line L2. Stance *boem soegi*,

cat stance. Technique *sonnal momtong makki*, mid-section twin knife-hand block.

12 With the right foot fixed, do *ap-chagi*, front kick, with the left foot, and drop it on the line L2. Land in *ap-koobi*, front stance, and do *momtong baro jireugi*, mid-section punch, reverse hand.

13 Pull the left foot in without moving the right. Stance *boem soegi*, cat stance. Technique *batang son momtong makki*, mid-section palm block.

14 Turn the body to the right to face the direction of R2. Form *boem soegi*, cat stance, facing R2. Technique *sonnal momtong makki*, mid-section twin knife-hand block.

15 With the left foot fixed, do *ap-chagi*, front kick, with the right foot and drop it on the line R2. Land in *apkoobi*, front stance, then do *momtong baro jireugi*, mid-section punch, reverse hand.

16 Pull in the right foot without moving the left. Form *boem soegi*, cat stance. Do *batang son momtong makki*, mid-section palm block.

17 With the left foot fixed, turn the body right and move the right foot to the line between G and I, facing G. Stance *dwit koobi*, back stance. Technique *geodeureo arae makki*, low-section guarding block.

18 Do *doobaldangsang ap-chagi*, front kick, with the left foot, then jumping front kick with the right foot, with *kiup*. Land in *apkoobi*, front stance, then do *momtong makki* followed by *momtong doobeon jireugi*, mid-section inner block followed by mid-section double punch.

19 Pivoting on the ball of the right foot, turn the body to the left and move the left foot to the line L1. Stance *dwit koobi*, back stance. Technique *hansonnal momtong bakat makki*, mid-section single knife-hand block.

20 Push the left foot forwards a little into *apkoobi*, front stance. Technique *palkoop eolgol dollyo chigi*, high-section elbow strike.

21 Keep both feet still. Technique *deung joomeok eolgol apchigi* then *momtong bandae jireugi*, high-section back-fist strike followed by mid-section reverse punch.

22 With the right foot fixed, turn to the left and pull the left foot in a little to form *dwit koobi*, back stance. Technique *hansonnal momtong bakat makki*, mid-section single knife-hand block.

23 Push the right foot forward on the line R1. Stance *ap-koobi*, front stance. Technique *palkoop eolgol dollyo chigi*, high-section elbow strike.

24 Keep both feet still. Technique *deung joomeok eolgol apchigi* then *momtong bandae jireugi*, high-section back-fist strike, then mid-section punch, reverse hand.

- Pull the left foot in and face I. Come into *choonbi* stance. Stay focused and alert.

ADVANCED FORMS

The *taeguek* forms above, with some regional variations, form the core of forms training for many students of tae kwon do, worldwide. Further forms learned by advanced students may be as follows.

1 *Ko-ryo*

The name Korea comes from *ko-ryo*, an ancient dynasty (AD 918–1392), which consistently resisted Mongolian aggression.

Ko-ryo form is a way of cultivating the strength that arises from conviction. The student should try to demonstrate confidence and a strong will with each movement.

2 *Keum-gang* (diamond)

Diamond is hard; perfect and clear; beautiful. The most beautiful mountain range in Korea is called *Keum-Gang-San*. In Buddhism, the perception that breaks off agony of mind is called *keum-gang*.

The form *keum-gang* moves to outline the Chinese character for 'mountain'. The movement of the practitioner should be based on a spiritual strength that is as beautiful as *Keum-Gang* mountain and is strong enough to be beyond distraction.

3 *Taebaek* (mountain)

A mythological account of the founding of Korea says that about 4,300 years ago Dangoon founded the nation in *Taebaek*, now Mount *Baekdoo*. This is the highest mountain in Korea and held sacred. Because the mountain reaches towards the sun, *taebaek* also means 'light'. Mt *Baekdoo* is a symbol of Korea.

Practising this form one should demonstrate the vigour and determination of the Korean people, and perform with the precision and agility of light.

4 *Pyongwon* (plain)

The plain is a broad open expanse; it can represent the level ground of ordinary life, but can also mean a sense of majestic scale. *Pyongwon* is the application of the 'providence of the plain', which welcomes man as a part of itself rather than challenging him to conquer it. 'In this form the student should demonstrate the majestic but friendly spirit of the vast plain' (Richard Chun, *Advancing in Tae Kwon Do*).

5 *Sipjin* (decimal)

Sipjin represents numeracy, and logic based on the ten fingers and therefore the number base ten. It symbolizes the human ability to develop logic and understanding.

The form *sipjin* outlines the Chinese character that means ten. To demonstrate the quality and potential of decimals, seek stability with every movement, giving change a systematic orderly progression.

6 *Jitae* (earth)

All life comes from, and all life returns to, earth. The earth is endlessly fruitful and completely accepting. Earth hides its greatest power deep within its hot core, only occasionally welling up in earthquakes or volcanoes. In *jitae* one should show power welling up from strong muscles, and a deep powerful core.

7 *Cheonkwon* (sky)

Sky is sacred; humans envy the birds' flight, in which they seem to become part of the sky. In *cheonkwon* one should demonstrate piety and awe, and a desire to strive like a high-flying bird.

8 *Hansoo* (water)

Water cannot be stopped because it can flow around anything in its path. It overcomes obstacles not by destroying them with a sudden burst of force, but with persistence. 'Like water, the strength of tae kwon do stems not from stubbornness and the refusal to yield, but rather from fluidity and adaptability. Hansoo emphasises this, so its strength must come from its fluidity' (Richard Chun, *Advancing in Tae Kwon Do*).

9 *Ilyo* (oneness)

Ilyo is the goal of spiritual life for Buddhists. To achieve *ilyo*, one must discard worldly desires and have complete faith, and complete unity of body and mind.

> The first step to freedom is to realise that the self has no reality; then it is easy to shed the desires that the self clings to.
>
> The ideal of tae kwon do is this state of Ilyo. It is a discipline in which you concentrate your attention on every moment and in doing so shed all worldly thoughts and preoccupations. The Ilyo form begins and ends at a centre, moving outward but eventually returning to its centre to achieve oneness. The spirit must be kept within the confines of the form, allowing no distraction. (Richard Chun, *Advancing in Tae Kwon Do*)

As is clear from the descriptions of these patterns, the concepts of the forms are elemental, fundamental, and emphasise the imperative human need to integrate fully with the physical universe. Practice of forms on an everyday basis may often be tedious or frustrating, but from time to time there are moments of the peace that come from glimpsing that integration:

> 'Is not the whole universe you?
> Where is there anyone that is not you?
> You are the soul of the Universe.
> You are the sun, the moon, and the stars, and you are shining everywhere'
>
> (Vivekenanda, *Jnana*).

7 SPARRING AND DESTRUCTION

SPARRING

As his or her skill in tae kwon do improves, the student undertakes prearranged sparring; one-for-one, two-for-two and three-for-three free sparring; and eventually completely unprogrammed free sparring. For some students this is the whole point of their studies – they love putting a series of techniques together into powerful, fluid sequences; they love the strategic dialogue between themselves and their opponents. A proportion of those students will want to extend that challenge into competition fighting; for a few of these, Olympic dreams will seem to be within their reach.

Prearranged sparring

We have already seen what profound concentration, what intense discipline and effort, is required to produce a correct technique in basic training or a correct sequence of techniques in pattern training, even though the opponent at that stage is an imaginary one. How is the student trained to move on to sparring, where the opponent is all too real? This is done stage by stage, beginning with prearranged sparring, sometimes known as technical sparring.

Students are paired up in two straight lines down the centre of the hall. They start at a distance from each other, so that if they both raise their arms to the front at solar-plexus level, with hands in fists, their knuckles will just touch.

At the teacher's command, students will come to attention, then bow to one another. One line will take one step back with the right foot into *apkoobi*, forward stance, *arae makki*, low block. The teacher will then describe the prearranged sparring sequence that he or she wants the students to practise.

An elementary sequence might be:

1 Attacking line (those in *apkoobi*, forward stance) take one step forwards in *apkoobi*, front stance, and do one *momtong bandae jireugi*, middle punch, with *kiup*. Defending line step one step back into *apkoobi*, front stance. Block the oncoming punch with *momtong an makki*, mid-section inner block, then do *momtong baro jireugi*, middle punch, reverse hand, to the solar plexus with *kiup*. Both lines return to *choonbi* position.

2 At the teacher's command, the attacking line takes one step back into *apkoobi*, front stance, doing *arae makki*, low block, with *kiup*. The attacking line moves one step forwards in *apkoobi*, front stance, executing one *momtong bandae jireugi*, mid-section punch, with *kiup*. The defending line moves one step back into *choochoom soegi*, horseriding stance, and blocks the oncoming punch with a *momtong bakat makki*, mid-section outer block. Students in this line then step the front foot a little to the right into *apkoobi*, front stance, and perform one *momtong baro jireugi*, mid-section reverse punch, to the solar plexus, with *kiup*. Both lines return to *choonbi* position.

3 At the teacher's command, the attacking line takes one step back into *apkoobi*, front stance, doing *arae makki*, low block, and *kiup*. The attacking line then moves one step forward, into *apkoobi*, front stance, executing one *momtong bandae jireugi*, middle punch, with *kiup*. The defending line takes one step back in *choochoom soegi*, horseriding stance, and blocks the oncoming punch with a *momtong bakat makki*, mid-section outer block. Moving the front leg across into *apkoobi*, front stance, draw the front arm back and perform *hansonnal anchigi*, outer knife-hand strike, with *kiup*, to the opponent's neck. Both lines return to *choonbi* position.

Students should then exchange roles, with the line that was attacking, defending, and *vice versa.*

A more advanced sequence might be:

1 At the teacher's command, the attacking line takes one step back with the right foot into *apkoobi,* front stance, doing *arae makki,* low block, with *kiup.* The attacking line takes one step forwards into *apkoobi,* front stance, and executes one *momtong bandae jireugi,* middle punch, with *kiup.* The defending line steps sideways into *choochoom soegi,* horseriding stance, and blocks the oncoming punch with *hansonnal makki,* knife-hand block. With the right foot, do *dollyo chagi,* turning kick, step down and turn to face the same direction as your opponent. With the left foot do a low sweep to destroy his or her footing, then pull the left foot into the body and finish with *dwi chagi,* low back-kick, to the falling opponent, and *kiup.* Both students return to *choonbi* position.

2 The attacking line steps back the right foot into *apkoobi,* front stance, doing *arae makki,* low block, with *kiup.* The attacking line then moves forwards one step into *apkoobi,* front stance, and executes one *momtong bandae jireugi,* middle punch, with *kiup.* The defending line steps the right foot back into *dwit koobi,* back stance, and does high-section knife-hand X-block to stop the oncoming punch. Then the defending student twists the attacker's forearm clockwise down to hip level, which causes the opponent to lean forwards. The defending line performs reverse downward knife-hand strike with *kiup* to neck. Both lines then return to *choonbi* position.

3 The attacking line takes one step back into *apkoobi,* front stance, with *arae makki,* low block, with *kiup.* The attacking line then takes one step forwards into *apkoobi,* front stance, and executes one *momtong bandae jireugi,* middle punch, with *kiup.* The defending line takes one step back with the right foot into *dwit koobi*, back stance, and does one *batang son momtong makki*, downward palm block, to stop the oncoming punch. With the back foot do a *bandal chagi*, high-section inward crescent kick. Continue turning, drop the foot one step behind the other foot, and do *bandae dollyo goro chagi*, high-section back-hook kick. Land in *dwit koobi*, back stance, guarding block. Both lines return to *choonbi* position.

Students should then exchange roles, with the line which was attacking, defending, and *vice versa*.

One-step technical or prearranged sparring should be practised in a precise manner, with each stance and each move crisp and clear, as in basic classical training drill.

This kind of training increases the student's capacity to move from one stance to another, keeping his or her balance, and altering the centre of gravity through legs and thighs when necessary, and allows them to begin to string together hand and foot techniques in increasingly complicated sequences. It also accustoms students to face an oncoming attack by a real opponent.

One-for-one sparring

Students will later be taught to engage in one-for one, two-for-two and three-for-three sparring, and 'stepping' exercises.

In one-for-one sparring, students stand in two lines facing one another. They will come to attention and bow, then step back the right foot into free sparring stance, and guarding block, with *kiup*.

The teacher may then instruct the students to do a particular kick each, such as *yop-chagi*, side kick, step back, on one side, and *dwi chagi*, back kick, return, on the other. Students will work together slowly at first, and speed up once they find their confidence. Students should work both sides of the body alternately, and alternate roles. This again speeds up students' technique and accustoms them to facing attacks from a 'real' opponent.

Alternatively, students may be told to spar one-for-one

freely. At first it is quite difficult even to think of which kicks to produce, but the student soon learns to perform a varied flow. At first you have to choose what kicks to do consciously, but this is slow. Later on the kicks seem to come from the unconscious, bypassing the processes of conscious decision; these are quicker, more powerful kicks. The student also begins to get a feeling of which kicks flow well into other kicks.

In one-for-one free sparring students simply perform one technique each alternatively. And slowly you begin to anticipate the technique your opponent is going to use. One-for-one also builds up stamina, as the rhythm eventually becomes very fast, with barely time to draw breath between one technique and the next.

One-for-one sparring can be extended to two-for-two and three-for-three, where each student executes two or three techniques while the opponent moves backwards, then *vice versa.* These exercises are less exhausting in the anaerobic sense, as there is time for recovery as you move backwards during your opponent's attacks. The exercises also allow students to experiment with different kicking combinations, and to become familiar with a real opponent bearing down on them with a determined fast set of combined techniques.

In one-for-one, two-for-two and three-for-three step sparring, students should *kiup* on each technique, and become familiar with the breath control and rhythm which this induces. *Kiup* also helps to reinforce the understanding of technique coming from deep in the hips, so that this is not lost in the increasing speed. Although there is no reason for style to become sloppy, once into sparring mode it is acceptable to alter the movement for maximum speed. This does not need to be done consciously, it happens automatically with practice.

'Stepping'

For stepping practice, students once more form two lines facing one another, come to attention and bow, and step right feet back into free sparring stance, with *kiup.* The teacher will then devise various combinations of attack and defence to be practised backwards and forwards across the *dojang*, with students alternating roles as they work their way from one side of the hall to the other. Sometimes a counter-attack is added to the sequence. For example the sequence could be:

- **Line A:** *dollyo chagi*, mid-section roundhouse kick, with the back foot, step forwards, turn backwards 180° and step forwards again, another *dollyo chagi*, mid-section roundhouse kick.
- **Line B:** replies with *dwi chagi*, back kick.

Students work slowly at first and then speed up as their confidence and accuracy improve.

This type of exercise helps the student get a feel for placing a kick accurately on an advancing opponent, and again provides experience on how to read an oncoming kick from an opponent's small pre-technique signs and movements. The student's footwork improves, as does his or her ability to control hip and torso position, angle and momentum. 'Stepping' exercises improve stamina, less in the 'sprint' manner of one-for-one sparring, and more in a middle-distance sense, building up moderate endurance.

All these sparring practices help to make the body quick to respond to attacks, and to make reflex or instinctive the fluent combinations of kicks that become the vocabulary of sparring.

Free sparring

Three-for-three sparring and 'stepping' practice may well, once the students are warmed up and animated, lead into spontaneous little bursts of free sparring. So long as this is considered appropriate by the instructor in terms of space and supervision, then this will be a good way to make the transition into free sparring itself.

Free sparring is completely unprogrammed sparring between partners, in which inventive combinations and good defences and counter-attacks are put together in sequences, with variations of rhythm. Versatility becomes the key quality.

Free sparring.

A training rhythm is crucial in class in order to maintain momentum and unformity. However, once free sparring begins, students must break out of all predictable rhythms and move away from any patterns that can be easily guessed or anticipated. Although light dancing on the feet and movement of the guarding fists are important in order to keep the body poised, in a state of potential movement, the participant in sparring needs to be aware of interrupting and syncopating this rhythm, otherwise his or her attacks will occur predictably on the beat.

Dummy kicks, feints and lunges can be used to assess the opponent's temperament and reactions, and then attacks launched at varied heights and from varied approaches – off the back leg; off the front leg; with a skip or side step; with a dummied spinning kick preceding it in order to move the opponent back and confuse him or her about which side the next attack will come from.

Watching real adepts sparring you will see fighters aiming their feet and legs with incredible precision to probe and unbalance their opponent's defences, and then go in with one or more clear attacks, to devastating effect.

In practice bouts in ordinary club fighting you will see fighters enjoying experimenting with each other and sometimes even smiling with pleasure at each other's expertise. At its best this sort of sparring is a good opportunity to share expertise; the more skilled person can challenge and stretch the less skilled, while perhaps feeling safe enough to try out some new combinations him or herself. But in another mood, or in the lead-up towards an important competition, even club sparring partners may want to fight more in earnest and push one another to their limits.

SAFETY

Safety must be a primary concern; in any sparring encounter both participants must exercise control. It will be specified by the class instructor whether the sparring is to be done with no contact, light contact or moderate contact.

Non-contact sparring is a valuable technical exercise in precision, time and style, and in sparring dialogue. However, anyone with aspirations to fight in tournaments should beware that it is likely that extensive non-contact training may train them to aim to miss.

Light contact practice ensures that your positioning and range is correct and clear, and begins to accustom you to landing and receiving blows.

For moderate contact sparring the *ho goo* (chest protector) should be worn, as well as shin guards and groin protectors. If the sparring partners want to move from fairly relaxed interplay to fierce and concentrated sparring with control but without other inhibition, they will probably benefit from the instructor or a responsible senior (especially one who has attended a refereeing course) overseeing their sparring and stopping them if the exchange becomes too fierce.

PAIRING

It is useful in club training if the pairing for sparring exercises is rotated so that students become accustomed to fighting with both more skilled and less skilled students, and adjusting accordingly. They also get used to a number of different body types, temperaments and rhythms. However, even if training is organized so that students regularly spar with every other person in the club, it is important to take any opportunity (properly uniformed, warmed up, and supervised, of course) to spar with unfamiliar partners.

Sometimes you might be paired with someone and get the eerie feeling that the person with whom you are sparring can read your mind and block all your techniques, almost before you have attempted them. This can arise for any one, or a combination, of three factors. The simplest answer is that your partner may be expert, highly trained and highly attuned, as any senior *dan* will probably be; he or she is so highly sensitive to what you are doing that they can anticipate what you are about to do without your being particularly obvious about it.

A second factor might be that, even if your opponent is not of high rank or particularly expert, you have fought one another many times before and therefore tend to have formed habitual sequences of response. You also have a sparring relationship; you make assumptions about who is stronger, who is fitter, and so forth. These habitual chain-reaction fighting sequences must be broken; although it may be awkward, you must always be ready to challenge and renegotiate a sparring relationship. A psychologically mature fighter will not object to a junior person or a less skilled person improving, and will never try to demoralize a sparring partner who is making unexpected strides.

The third possibility, when you are apparently having your mind read, is that you are telegraphing – making recognizable pre-technique gestures or grimaces which clearly signal the effort you are about to make, and, often, the side of the body that you are going to use. Students with whom you train can be a great help in pointing this out – and you can guard against it yourself by trying to keep your face impassive and soft, except when doing a *kiup*, and by moving smoothly into techniques, gathering the necessary *ki* quietly from within, rather than with the visible bunching of muscles characteristic of so many Western physical training disciplines.

COMPETITION TAE KWON DO

Many students of tae kwon do want to spar on a competitive basis with other clubs, on a local, national or international basis, and of course many extend their longing towards the Olympic competition. Some clubs are highly geared up for competition training, regularly training in body armour and participating in competitions, while others only occasionally include sparring with any degree of contact in their training programmes, and hardly ever field teams at tournaments. Indeed, there is considerable tension within tae kwon do as to exactly where the 'right' path lies; whereas in some clubs sparring and tournament fighting is the goal to which all other training aims, in others it is only an equal element alongside all the other aspects of training.

For a start, there is a philosophical problem about 'winning'. If a fighter wins a tournament, what does that mean? Does that make him or her a better martial artist, or is it simply a peripheral event during their training? What can the concept of 'winning' mean in the martial art ethic? What does it mean when texts about tae kwon do refer to 'athletes' or 'fighters', rather than 'students' and 'artists'?

The confident tournament fighter may feel that the moral and philosophical reservations professed by martial artists who don't frequent tournaments are simply rationalizations, a way of avoiding their own fears of 'real' combat. Perhaps sometimes doubts and reservations are a cloak for fear, but without doubt they are sometimes deeply felt.

Ken Singleton, a distinguished *karateka*, makes the following point about the (disappointingly sparse) television coverage of tae kwon do at the Seoul Olympics:

> No medals were at stake, but presumably to satisfy the requirements of competition there were winners and losers and competitors fought for points and half points as they do in all martial arts tournaments. The only piece of televised action broadcast in Britain showed a young man writhing on the floor having been kicked between the legs. It formed part of a lighthearted round-up of less-fortunate competitors' setbacks during the day – horses throwing riders over fences, a diver hitting his head on the springboard and others whose mistakes were picked up by cameras and relayed to the world. Beneficial it may be in terms of television viewer ratings, but Tae Kwon Do will live in the minds of the layman as being a 'sport' where young men with no control kick each other. (Ken Singleton, *An Introduction to Karate*)

Perhaps this highlights an important point: that tae kwon do must look after its public image, whatever path and emphasis it chooses, because the media will trivialize and sensationalize anything they can, given half a chance.

Some tae kwon do commentators have suggested that the two paths of sport and art are already so far apart that a split is inevitable (see Sang Kyn Shim, *Tae Kwon Do Times*, May 1990), while others (see Moo Yong Lee's answering editorial, *Tae Kwon Do Times*, September 1990) feel that integration of the two activities is possible, and is indeed the better way forward: 'Take time to speak with WTF competitors at any level. What you'll find, almost without exception, is superior sportsmanship and a real spirit of mutual respect among opponents. They are, above all, brothers and sisters in Tae Kwon Do.'

Over the next 10 or 20 years, and partly dependent on what the Olympic future for tae kwon do holds, this debate between the opposite poles will develop and may be resolved. The way forward at this moment would seem to be open and mutually respectful discussion between all those involved.

WTF competition tae kwon do is organized and formalized in the following ways:

- For international competitions the ring is a square with 12-metre sides around the outer boundary, and a square with 8 metre sides around the inner boundary. For regional and local tournaments the outer square has sides of 8 metres and the inner square has sides of 6 metres. The floor of the inner square must be flat, and either wooden or covered in foam padding.
- Contestants must wear the standard white uniform, clean, pressed and in good order, and must wear approved headgear, *ho goo* (chest protector), forearm and shin pads, and a groin protector. The contestants' nails must be short, and long hair must be tied back with a rubber band only (metal clips may fly out and injure either competitor). All watches and jewellery must be removed.
- No non-prescribed drugs or intoxicants are to be used before or during the match; any competitor doing so is automatically disqualified.
- The valid targets are on the front of the body between the area of the opponent's waist and the base of the neck (but not the throat). Foot techniques are allowed to the head. Hand techniques are not allowed to the head, and open-hand techniques are not allowed at all. To score, a technique must land with sufficient impact to cause a visible shock to the body.
- All competitions are supervised by one referee, four judges, two jurors, a timekeeper and a recorder. All these officials must be qualified. There is an internationally agreed set of signals and gestures with which the referee indicates points awarded, penalties, stoppages, counts, transgressions of specific rules (holding the opponent, avoiding fighting by turning back, etc.) and declaring the winner.
- If the score on techniques at the end of a match is a tie,

a decision is made on the following bases:

1 A technique that has caused a knock down of a count of eight or more is superior to any other technique.
2 Any foot technique is superior to any hand technique.
3 Any jumping technique is superior to any standing technique.
4 Any kick to the head is superior to any kick to the body.
5 Any counter-attack is superior to any initiated attack.
6 If these criteria do not give a result, whichever fighter was more aggressive wins the match.

The weight categories for tournament fighting

Category	*Men* kg (lb)		*Women* kg (lb)	
Fin	Under 50	(110.0)	Under 43	(94.6)
Fly	50–54	(110.0–118.5)	43–47	(94.6–103.4)
Bantam	54–58	(118.5–127.6)	47–51	(103.4–112.2)
Feather	58–64	(127.6–140.8)	51–55	(112.2–121.0)
Light	64–70	(140.8–154.0)	55–60	(121.0–130.0)
Welter	70–76	(154.0–167.2)	60–65	(130.0–143.0)
Middle	76–83	(167.2–182.6)	65–70	(143.0–154.0)
Heavy	Over 83	(182.6)	Over 70	(154.0)

BREAKING TECHNIQUES

Breaking techniques are used to test and demonstrate the power, speed and focus of techniques. And without a doubt they are also exhilarating – anyone who saw the opening ceremony for the 1988 Olympic Games will remember the wonderful spray of broken boards flying up and out of the complex formations of the huge tae kwon do demonstration team.

Breaking techniques work, essentially, because the velocity of the hand or foot strike causes the hand or foot to have no time to 'deform', i.e. get squashed and therefore

Breaking.

injured, on impact. Without 'deforming', the hand or foot behaves like a hard rigid object and passes straight through the more brittle material (wood, brick or tiles) through which it is directed. Thus speed of technique is one essential factor, the other two being accuracy and power. All three can be developed first of all by learning correct technique; with correct technique breaking can be performed with apparent ease, where the use of brute force and ignorance will only result in injury. Once the technique is learned clearly and precisely, power and accuracy can be developed by practising on a punch bag, or a target pad on the floor for downward strikes on to horizontal targets. This accustoms the body to making powerful strikes with pinpoint accuracy; and, in the case of a strike with a very small impact area, for instance ridge-hand strike, you can repeatedly ensure that it is actually the ridge-hand itself that strikes the punch bag.

Good breathing is essential for successful breaking, a steady rhythm of diaphragmatic breathing being particularly important; when doing something potentially nerve-wracking like this you must consciously avoid shallow anxious breathing. You should get into the correct stance near the target, measure up once or twice to ensure that the strike will land correctly, then collect your thoughts and *ki. Kiup* once to let the people holding the board know that the technique is imminent, or, in the case of a downward strike, simply to marshal your own concentration, then *kiup* again with the technique, this second *kiup* coming spontaneously.

With precise technique, and attention to and practice on speed and power, there is no need to build up thick skin and callouses on the hands and feet; indeed that type of conditioning seems to be an unnecessary abuse of the body, and counter to the spirit of caring for and enhancing the body which is central to tae kwon do.

When doing a break, particularly one that feels challenging, a strange effect occurs, whereby once into the breaking sequence, you can neither hear nor see anything peripheral, and the world seems to shrink into the stack of roof tiles, or whatever. You do not feel the strike; you are more aware of the *kiup*, and then wake up, as if from a daze, looking at a highly satisfactory heap of rubble. Certainly the first few times you manage something like this, it releases a great deal of energy, and you can feel quite high.

Public demonstrations of tae kwon do often include elaborately staged breaks, including leaps over motorbikes, jumping spinning back-hook and reverse crescent kicks, and other exciting material; but even at club level, you can learn the simple elements of how to break. However, no one should attempt to learn breaking without proper supervision, as serious injury would be almost inevitable. The instructor will decide when the time is right for each person, and how they ought to begin.

As well as being enjoyable, breaking is a part of many grading tests and an element of basic training that gives an opportunity to check on accuracy and technique.

8 CLASS AND GRADING

CLASS ROUTINE

On entering the *dojang* for class, any student, visitor or observer, indeed any instructor, bows to show respect for the art. Whenever one leaves and re-enters the room one bows again, until finally bowing out at the end of the session.

Bags, coats and clutter should be left in changing rooms; if that is not possible, or is not considered safe, all the clutter should be restricted to as small a space as possible. Ideally, there should be no clock, or any clock should be covered up, since it is very difficult, if you can see the time, not to try to pace yourself through the class – where, in essence, not only should you be doing every technique with total commitment, but also, if necessary, you can stop before the end of class if you are exhausted. However, not looking at the clock could be a good piece of self-discipline for all students training in a hall where there is one.

At the beginning of class, junior students will be detailed to sweep the floor; it is important not to have any grit or debris on the floor as this can be very painful on the feet, and also can flick up into students' eyes. Until the instructor calls the class to order students may chat quietly or do some stretching on their own, but as soon as the training begins the talking has to stop and everything must be done with full concentration and commitment.

A warm-up often begins with running round the hall for a few minutes, to raise the pulse rate and to begin to wake up the breathing and the muscles. To increase agility the running may include side-stepping, twist-stepping, running backwards, zigzag running through the circle of other students and short sprints. Exercises like leap-frogs, hopping and so on may also be included.

There is a huge variety of stretching, strengthening and refining exercises, and the instructor will select the variety that he or she finds the most appropriate. Usually there will be a core of exercises that is always undertaken so that strength and flexibility have a chance to improve, and sets of other exercises that can be used in rotation. The warm-up will probably last a good 20 minutes to half an hour; tae kwon do technique itself is so demanding that the body really must be warmed well through before one begins.

After warming up, there will be so much to do that an hour-and-a-half or even a two-hour training session will be barely time enough to cover the syllabus. Often, therefore, one training session a week will tend to concentrate on sparring, and the other on patterns, and learning new kicks, strikes and forms.

Students who are still building their strength and stamina, or who have missed training because of holidays or illness, will probably experience a wave of exhaustion at several points during the class. But anyone can bow out of a class at any time without being challenged as to why; indeed, sometimes it is essential to do so. However, you will often find that if you can hang on during the wave of nausea or tiredness, after a few more minutes you will begin to feel much better, more powerful and fit.

Basic technique, forms, prearranged and free sparring will all be covered regularly, senior students frequently being detailed to teach small groups of juniors. The class will then finish with cooling-down exercises – generally loosening and stretching, and sometimes massage, though some instructors like to include a final burst of stamina training in the last few minutes.

At the end of class, again, students may linger for a while going over technique or chatting, but usually the *dojang* has to be cleared and locked fairly promptly, and students must leave. It is wonderful if you train somewhere where there are efficient hot showers, since you will sweat profusely during class. One soldier, who trains new recruits for the army and is therefore no slouch, declared that he sweated more in the tae kwon do *dojang* than at any other kind of training he had ever undertaken. Men and women practitioners with long hair will be amazed to find their hair soaked with sweat after training, and everyone finds their uniform is wet and clinging by the end of class. So, showered or not, it is of vital importance to put on extra layers of track suit, sweatshirts, or similar garments before going out into the night air, or you are likely to suffer from aching muscles and chills.

GRADINGS

Students of tae kwon do tie a belt over the tunic of their *dobok*, the colour of the belt denoting their rank. The white and coloured belts are the *kup* or student grades, while the black belts denote *dan* or teacher grades. At the beginning of class, students line up according to the seniority of their grades, with the most senior student being on the front right-hand corner of the group as one faces the front.

The sequence of colours is:

- 12th *kup*, white belt.
- 11th *kup*, white belt, one yellow tag.
- 10th *kup*, white belt, double yellow tag.
- 9th *kup*, yellow belt.
- 8th *kup*, yellow belt, one green tag.
- 7th *kup*, yellow belt, double green tag.
- 6th *kup*, green belt.
- 5th *kup*, green belt, blue tag.
- 4th *kup*, blue belt.
- 3rd *kup*, blue belt, red tag.
- 2nd *kup*, red belt.
- 1st *kup*, red belt, black tag.
- 1st *dan*, black belt.

The white belt represents beginning, innocence and purity; on the 'whiteness' or ignorance of the student will gradually be 'written' meanings and techniques. Coloured tags are the transitional grades between the colours, signifying that the student is moving from one stage to the next.

- The yellow of yellow belt represents the earth, in which things grow.
- The green of green belt is the new growth the student experiences once he or she has reached that stage.
- Blue signifies the sky; students at blue-belt level are 'reaching for the sky'.
- Red is the colour that warns of danger; red belt is the dangerous level. The student knows a wide range of devastating techniques, but does not necessarily always understand the best way to employ and control them. For this reason, red belt is probably the most risky stage for injuries.

Black belt is the first *dan* grade. Black is the opposite of white, and balances white in the yin/yang symbol; it signifies that the student has completed the first cycle of learning. Being an absence of colour, and therefore, in a way, analogous to white, the black belt also signifies a kind of return to innocence.

All through the *kup* grades students long for a black belt, but, once attained, most practitioners say they feel very much like beginners again, as if only then are they ready to start learning, in the same way that it is only once you have passed your driving test that you can start to learn to drive properly. It is also inadvisable to become fixed on the dream of having a black belt as though it was the be-all and end-all of training; C.W. Nicol made this mistake early on in his karate training:

> One morning at the Karate dojo, I asked Takagi Sensei how long it would take me to get a black belt. He looked up at me, stood, went from behind the desk and opened up the big cupboard where they kept the uniforms. He took out a brand new black belt.
>
> 'You want this?'
>
> I faltered, knowing that I had said something wrong. Then he threw the belt at me.

> 'Take this black belt and go back to your country!' . . .
>
> After that little lesson from Takagi Sensei I resolved never to put on a black belt unless I won the grade, and I never asked again about a black belt. (C.W. Nicol, *Moving Zen – Karate as a Way to Gentleness*)

A black belt has no meaning at all without the journey, with all its pitfalls and struggles, that leads to it. Having said that, though, if you are training on average twice a week there will usually be a three or four month gap between each grading. Some organizations insist on six months between red belt and black tag, with another six months or even a year between black tag and black belt. Once the practitioner has moved into the *dan* grades the intervals are a minimum of 18 months between first and second *dan*, and two years between second and third *dan*s. Two or three years must elapse between the third and fourth *dan* examinations.

Exams

The grading examiner for the *kup* grades must be at least a fifth *dan*, who is entitled to grade up to and including third *dan*. For gradings above third *dan*, a panel of seventh *dan*s is needed.

For a grading examination the senior instructor sits at a table, with notes on the students, and a senior student will assist by giving the necessary instructions to the students. The junior grades take the exam first, moving up through the grades in order of increasing seniority. Students must demonstrate familiarity with, and skill in, the material on their syllabuses; usually they will be asked to perform basic hand and foot techniques, patterns, one-step pre-arranged sparring and free sparring, and possibly a breaking technique, according to what they have studied and learned in class.

It is quite extraordinary how nervous some students get while taking their grading tests, and yet others seem unaffected by nerves and take the whole thing in their stride. Personally, I notice weird effects, like the soles of my feet being wet with panic-stricken sweat, and a feeling that I am making peculiar movements ('Why am I doing *an makki* like that? I've never done it like that before'). And I am not the only one:

> A friend of mine, a scientist in a controversial field, a master of the cool comeback in public debate, once told me of going completely blank during his brown belt exam: 'When my teacher called out the first technique, I simply didn't know what he was talking about. I heard words in a foreign language that didn't make any sense at all. So I just stood there, and when my *uke* came in with an attack – a strike to the top of the head – I just grabbed his hand and started grappling with him. It wasn't Aikido. It was survival. My teacher suggested I try the technique again and it was even worse. Then he called out the next technique. By this time, I didn't know who I was or where I was. I had never heard of Aikido. I looked around and wondered, who are these strange people dressed in white suits? Why are they sitting in this weird way? (George Leonard, *Aikido and the New Warrior*)

If you are one of the people who does become very nervous at gradings, all this is not intended to feed your hysteria, simply to show that it is a common problem.

Performing patterns at gradings is a very good test indeed, since you cannot consciously remember them under that kind of pressure; they have to be completely internalized. To overcome nerves, steady your breathing, and simply take the test, one item at a time. Discipline yourself not to worry about the patterns during basic techniques, or about sparring during patterns. Just do each technique to the best of your ability, one moment at a time, and the hard work you have put in during the weeks of training will shine through, even though at the time you fear that it will not.

Exam results are written into the student's grading record. If successful, the student is immediately entitled to put on either the next colour tag or the next colour belt. Taking due care not to make winning the next belt an aim or an end in itself, even those, or perhaps especially those, who find the grading itself very daunting feel an amazing sense of satisfaction after all has gone well and it is time to change the colour of the belt.

GLOSSARY

Since there is no standard system for transliterating Korean, the English spellings of Korean words are not definitive.

anchigi Strike travelling inwards towards the centre line of the opponent's body.
an makki Inner block.
ap-chagi Front kick.
apchigi Frontal strike.
apkoobi Forward stance.
apsoegi Walking stance.
arae makki Low-section block.
bakat Out or outer.
bakat chigi Outer form strike.
bakat makki Outer block.
bal Foot.
bandal chagi Crescent kick.
bandal sonnal chigi Reverse knife-hand strike.
baro Return to previous position or beginning.
baro jireugi Reverse punch.
batang son chigi Palm thrust.
boem soegi Tiger/cat stance.
budo The way of the warrior.
chagi Kick.
charyot soegi Attention stance.
chigi Strike.
chi jireugi Uppercut strike.
chodan First *dan*, first black-belt grade.
choochoom soegi Horseriding stance.
choonbi Ready stance.
daeryon Sparring.
dangyo teok Uppercut punch.
danjun Energy centre below the navel.
deemyun bandae dollyo jireugi Jumping reverse turning kick.

deemyun dollyo apchagi Jumping turning kick.
deung joomeok apchagi Back-fist strike.
do Way of life; Way.
dobok Training uniform.
dojang Training hall.
dollyo Turning; roundhouse.
dollyo chagi Roundhouse or turning kick.
doobaldangsang Flying kick using both feet to hit the same target.
doobeon Double.
dora About face.
dwi chagi Back kick.
dwiro chigi Backward elbow strike.
dwit koasoegi Cross stance.
dwit koobi Back stance.
eolgol High section.
eolgol makki Upper block.
eotgoreo makki Block.
geuman Finish; conclude.
gooleo chagi Flying front kick.
haktari soegi Crane stance.
han Short for *hanna*, one.
hansonnal Single knife-hand.
hechyo makki Spread block.
ho goo Chest protector worn while sparring.
hwarang The 'flower of youth'; an elite warrior group of the Silla kingdom.
ilbo daeryon One-step sparring.
ilyo One-ness; unity; integration.
jayoo daeryon Free sparring.
jiptjung Using the breath to integrate the internal with the external.
jireugi Punch.
joomeok Fist.
keupso The body's vital parts.
ki Inner strength and power.
kiup A shout that collects and focuses internal energy.
kyungye Bow.
makki Block.

mit joomeok chigi Hammer-fist strike.
modeumbal Drawing the feet together.
mok Arm.
momdollyo chagi Spinning back kick.
momtong Mid section.
mooreup Knee.
myung chi Solar plexus.
naeryo Downwards.
naeryo chigi Downward punch.
naeryo jireugi Downward thrust.
naeryo makki Downward block.
ollyo chigi Upward elbow strike.
oreum Right.
otkolo makki Double fist X-block.
palgwe A series of patterns illustrating the eight trigrams of the *I Ching.*
palinok Forearm or wrist.
palkoop Elbow.
palkoop chigi Elbow strike.
parro Return to *choonbi.*
poomse Patterns.
pyeonhi Ready.
pyonson keut sewjireugi Spear-hand thrust to the solar plexus.
sabom Instructor.
sabomnim Instructor who is above fourth *dan.*
sewo jireugi Vertical punch.
shijak Begin.
simsa Grading.
soegi Stance.
sonkeut Fingertip.
sonnal Knife-hand.
sonnal deung Ridge-hand.
taeguek Series of eight basic patterns.
wen Left.
yop Side.
yop-chagi Side kick.
yop jireugi Side punch.
yop makki Side block.

NUMBERS AND COUNTING

hanna one
dul two
set three
net four
dasot five
yaset six
elgub seven
yodol eight
ahob nine
yol ten

il first
i second
sam third
sah fourth
oh fifth
yuk sixth
chill seventh
pal eighth
koo ninth
sib tenth

FURTHER READING

PHILOSOPHY

Zen Culture, Thomas Hoover, Wildwood House, 1977.
The Art of Strategy, Sun Tsu, trans. R.L. Wing, Aquarian Press, 1988.
Tao Te Ching, Lao Tzu, trans. GiaFuFeng and Jane English, Wildwood House, 1973.
Returning to Silence, Dainin Katagiri, Shambhala, 1988.
Effortless Being: Yoga Sutras of Patanjali, trans. Alistair Shearer, Thorsons, 1982.
The Upanishads, trans. Alistair Shearer and Peter Russell, Thorsons, 1978.
The Bhagavad Gita, trans. E. Easwaran, Arkana, 1989.
Zen Flesh, Zen Bones, Paul Reps, Penguin, 1957.
Zen and the Art of Calligraphy, Sogen and Katsujo, trans. Sterens, Arkana, 1983.
Stand Your Ground, Kaleghl Quinn, Orbis, 1983.

MARTIAL ARTS

Tae Kwon Do, Pack, Pack and Gerard, Facts on File, 1989.
Tae Kwon Do, Eddie Ferrie, Crowood, 1989.
Official WTF Tae Kwon Do, David Mitchell, Stanley Paul, 1986.
Tae Kwon Do, Richard Chun, Harper & Row, 1976.
Advancing in Tae Kwon Do, Richard Chun, Harper & Row, 1982.
The Art of Zen Archery, Hans Joachim Stein, Element, 1988.
Aikido and the New Warrior, ed. Heckler, North Atlantic Books, 1985.
An Introduction to Karate, Ken Singleton, Macdonald Optima, 1989.

Full Contact Karate, Jean Yves Thériault, Contemporary Books, 1983.
Moving Zen – Karate as a Way to Gentleness, C.W. Nicol, P.R. Crompton, 1981.
An Introduction to T'ai Chi, Alan Peck, Macdonald Optima, 1990.
T'ai Chi Ch'uan, Horwitz and Kimmelman, Rider, 1979.
The Essence of T'ai Chi, Lo, Inn, Amacker and Foe, North Atlantic Books, 1979.

FITNESS

Stretch and Relax, Maxine Tobias and Mary Stewart, Dorling Kindersley, 1985.
Hard Bodies Express Workout, Gladys Portugues and Joyce Vedral, Thorsons, 1988.
Post Natal Exercises, Margie Polden and Barbara Whiteford, Century, 1984.

BREATHING

Light on Pranayama, B.K.S. Iyengar, Thorsons, 1981.
Pranayama, André van Lysbeth, Thorsons, 1979.

BACKGROUND

A New History of Korea, Ki-Baik Lee, Seoul Harvard, 1984.
A Panorama of 5000 Years: Korean History, A.C. Nahon-Hollym, 1983.
Queen of Suffering: A Spiritual History of Korea, Ham Sok Hon, Friends World Committee, 1985.
Flowers of Fire: 20th Century Korean Stories, ed. Peter Lee, University of Hawaii Press, 1986.
Holidays in Hell, P.J. O'Rourke, Picador, 1988.

INDEX

Page numbers in *italic* refer to the illustrations